Coloring Trees: 40 Beautiful Tree Patterns for Adults

A BOOK BY

ZEN SKY COLORING

LET'S US BEGIN ☺

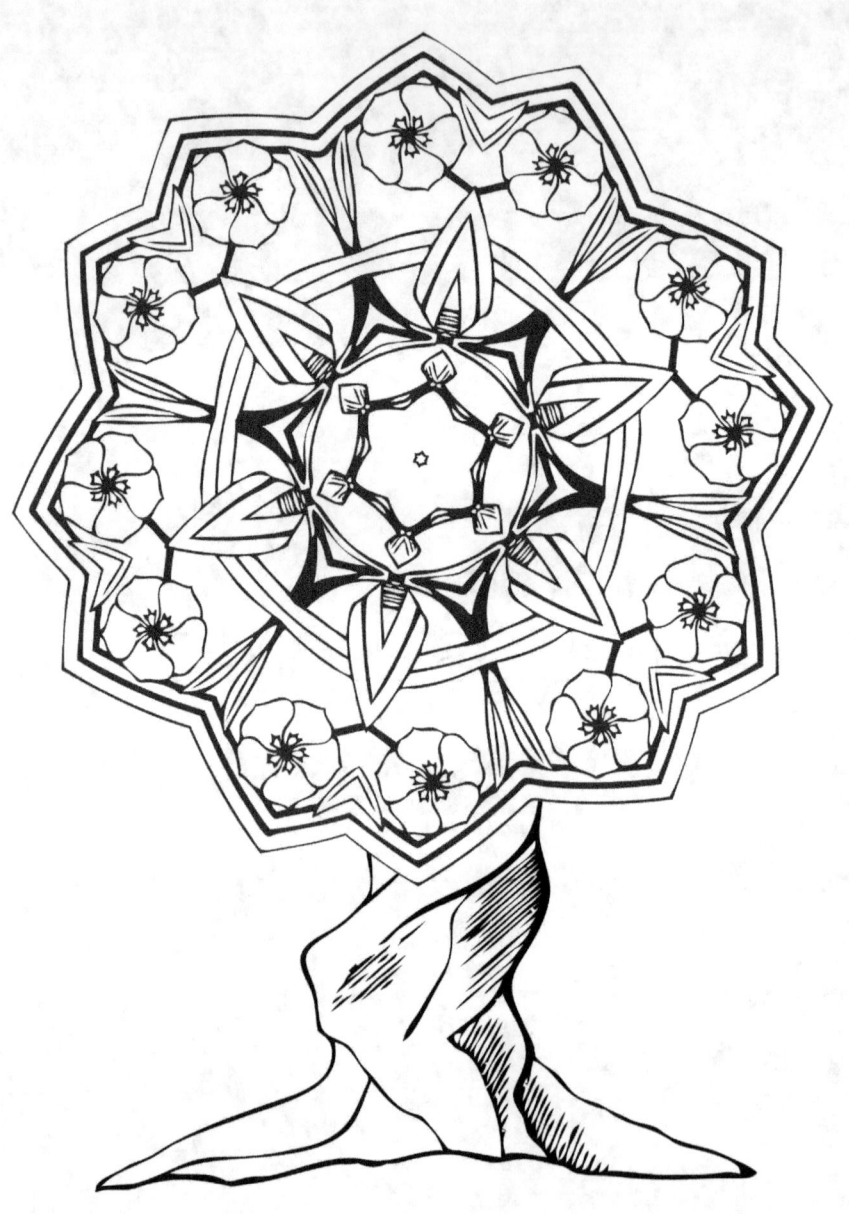

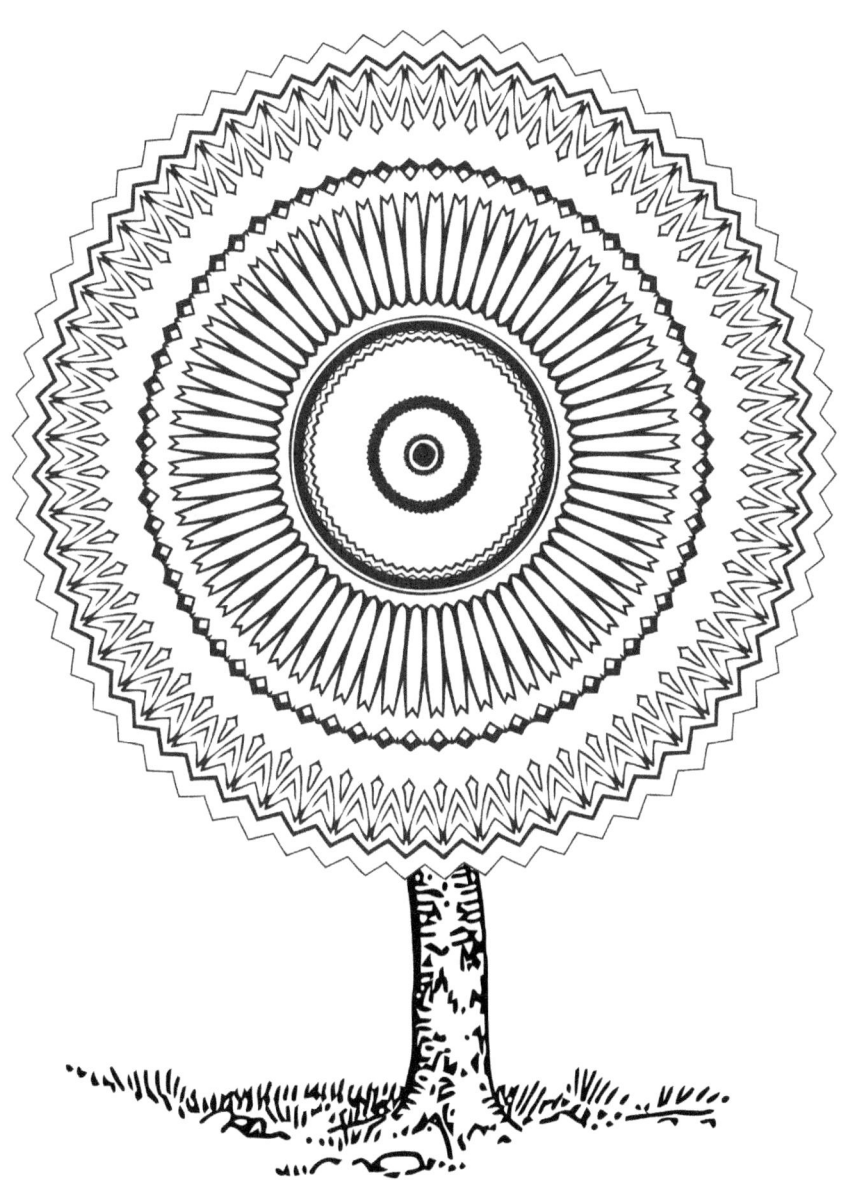

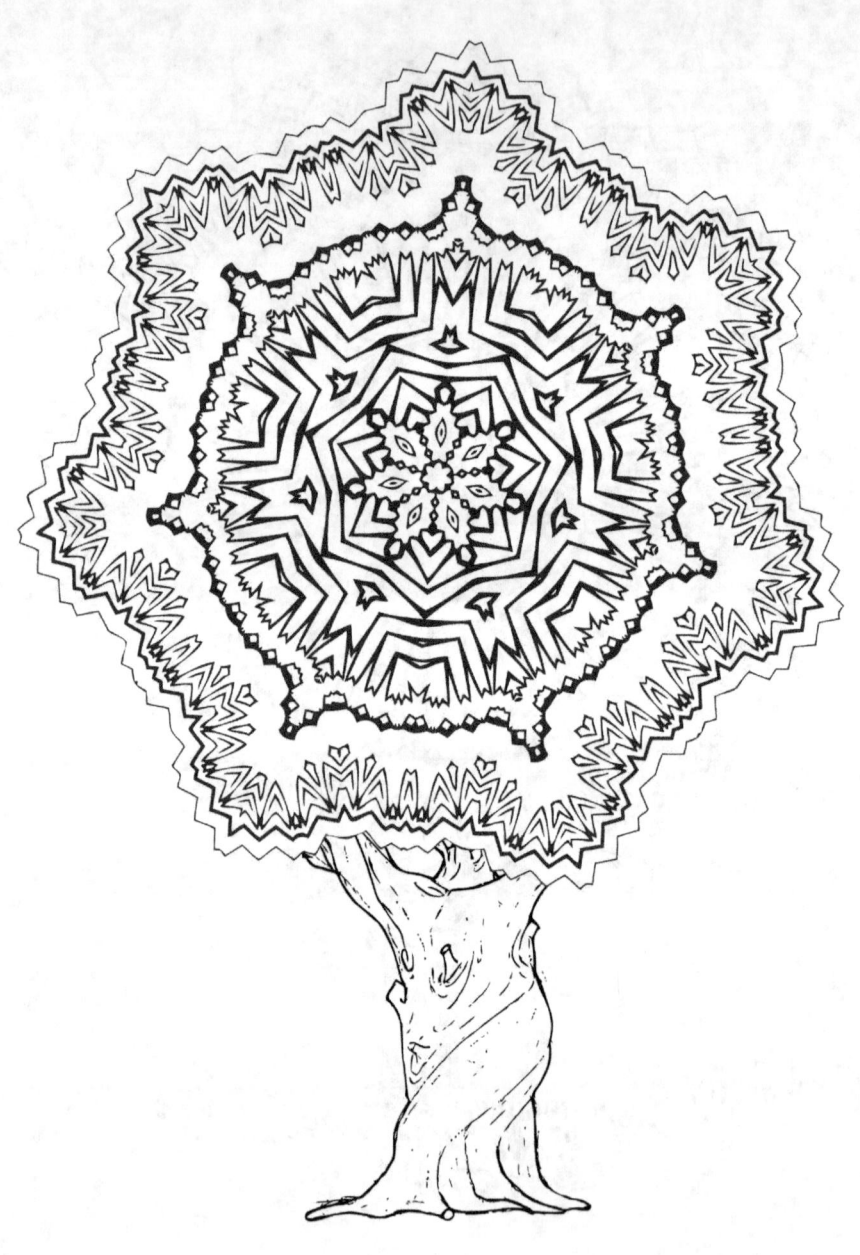

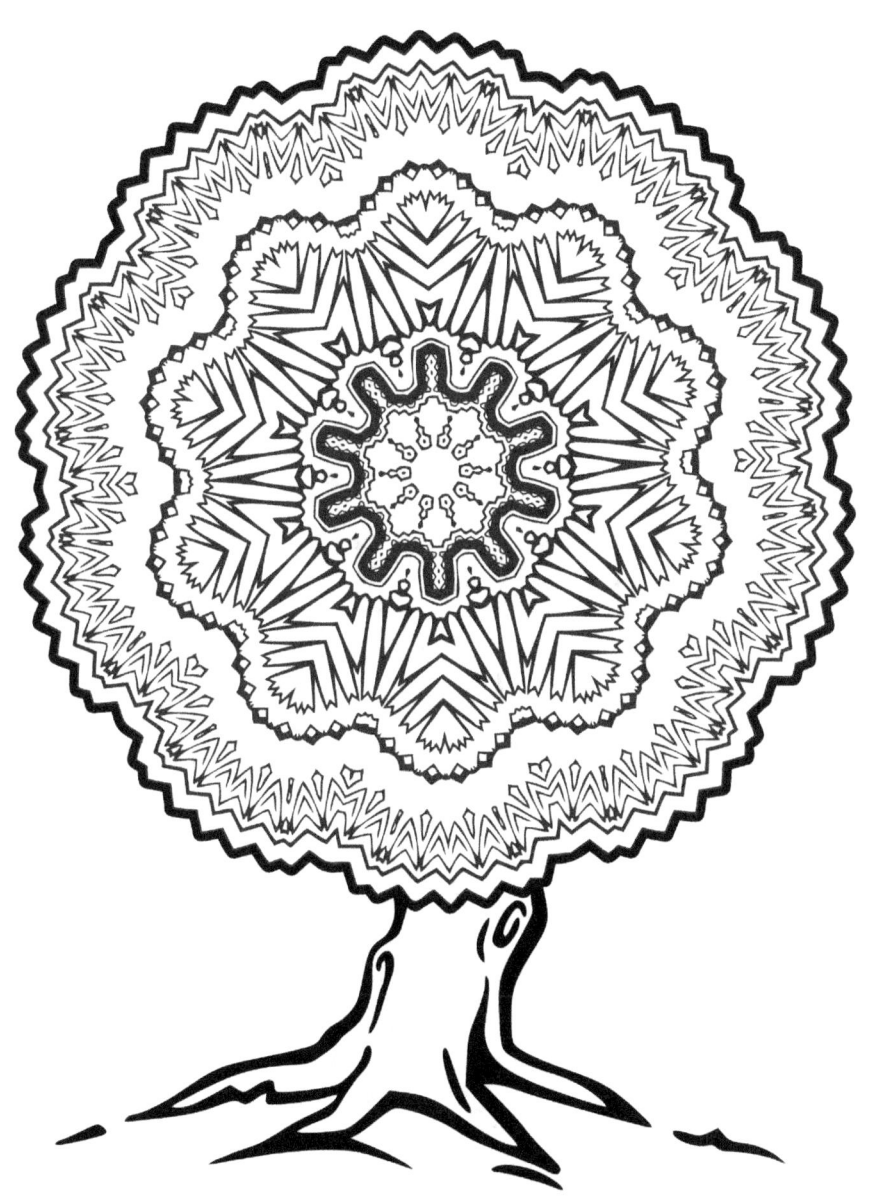

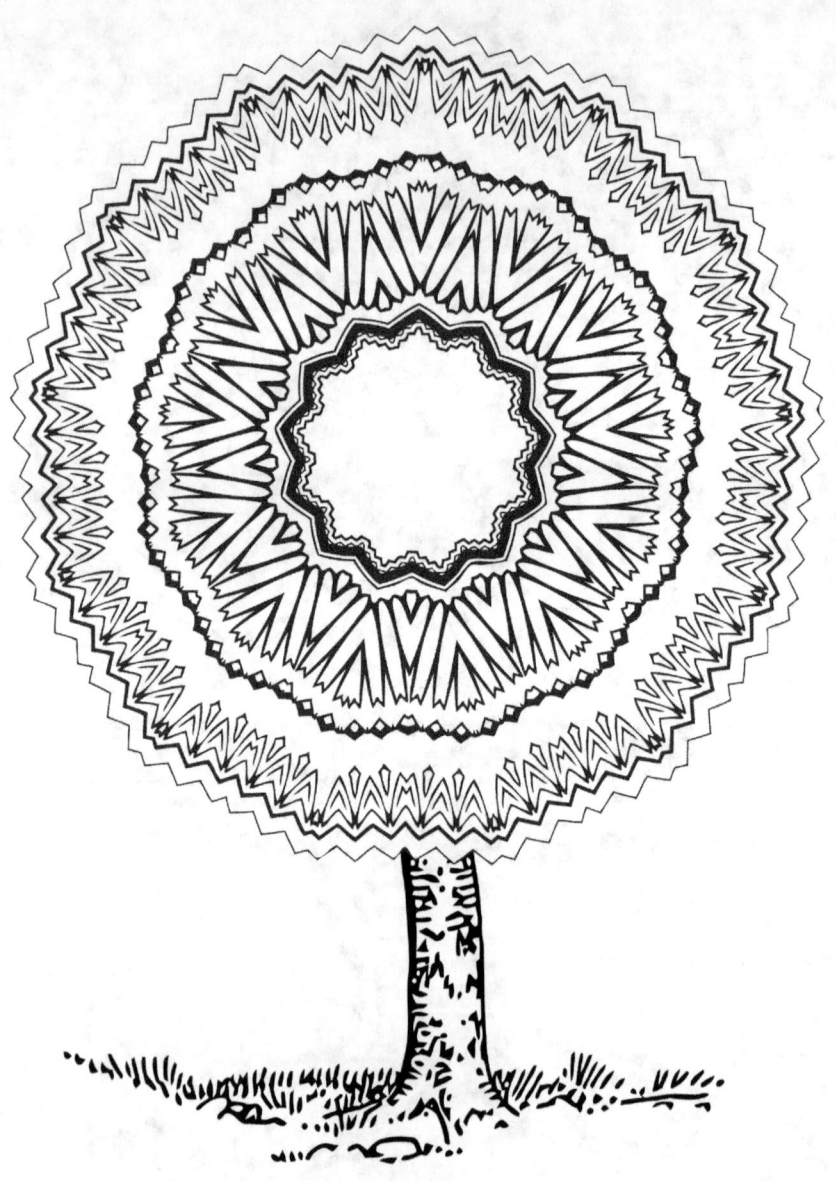

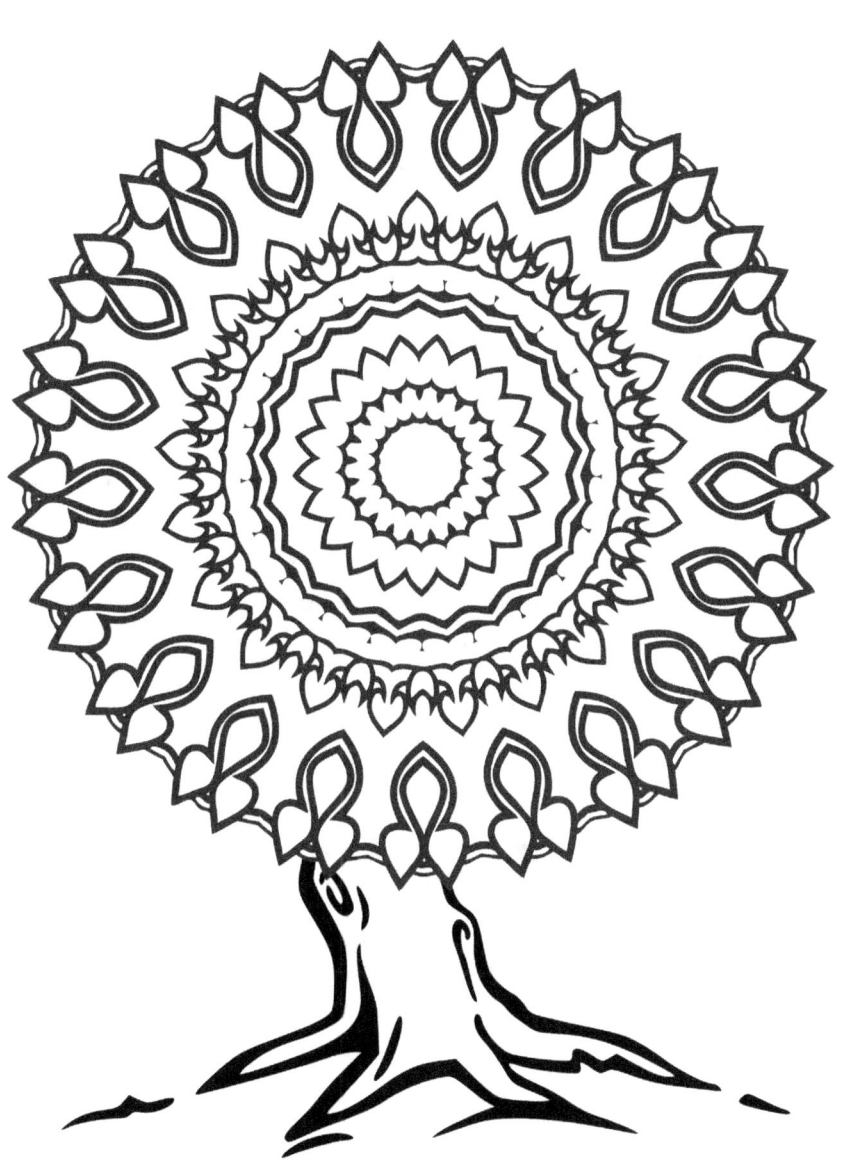

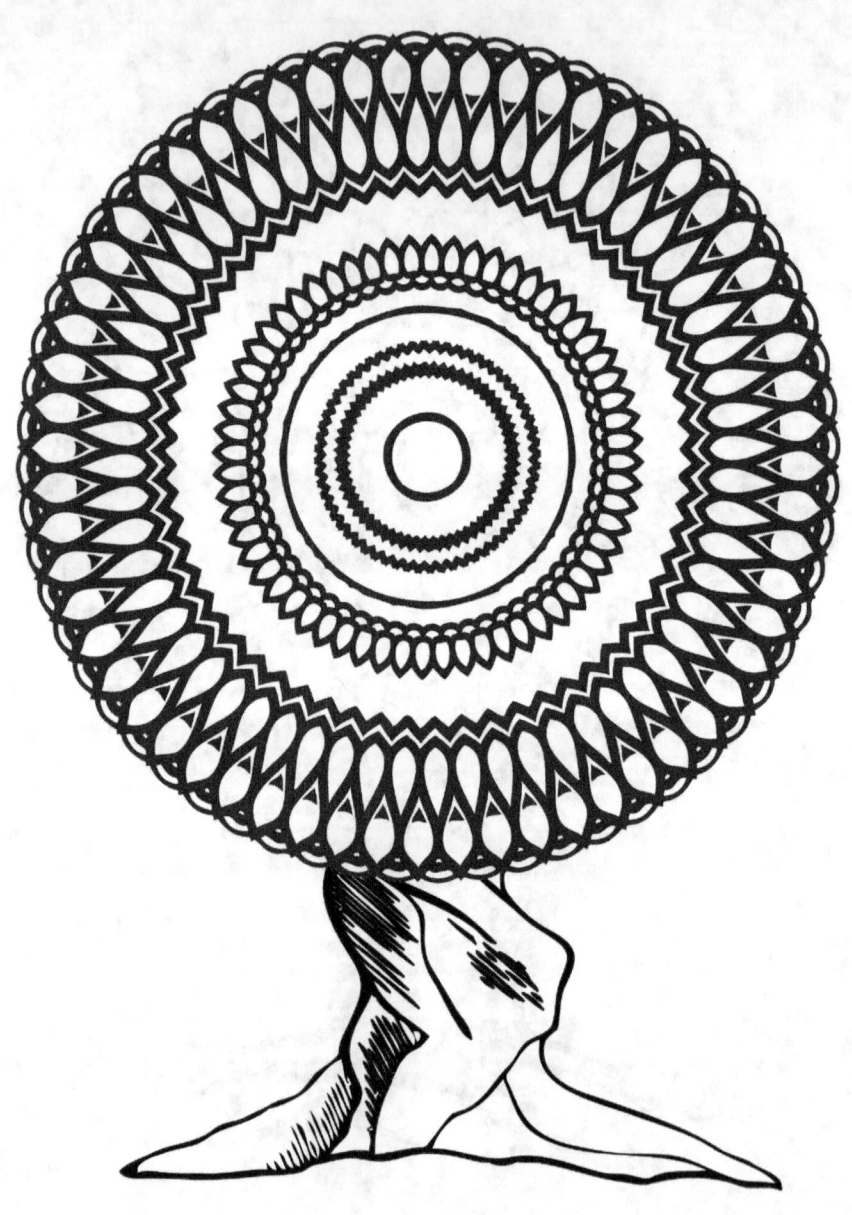

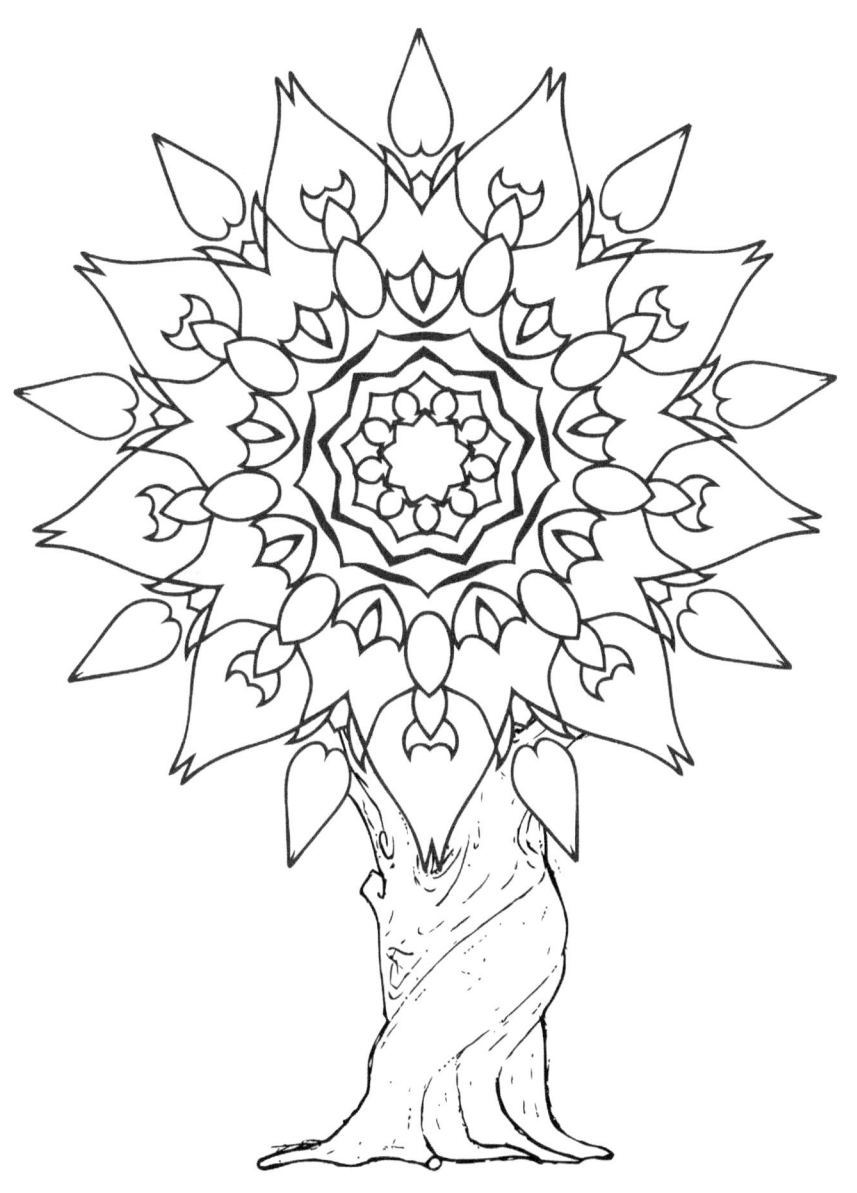

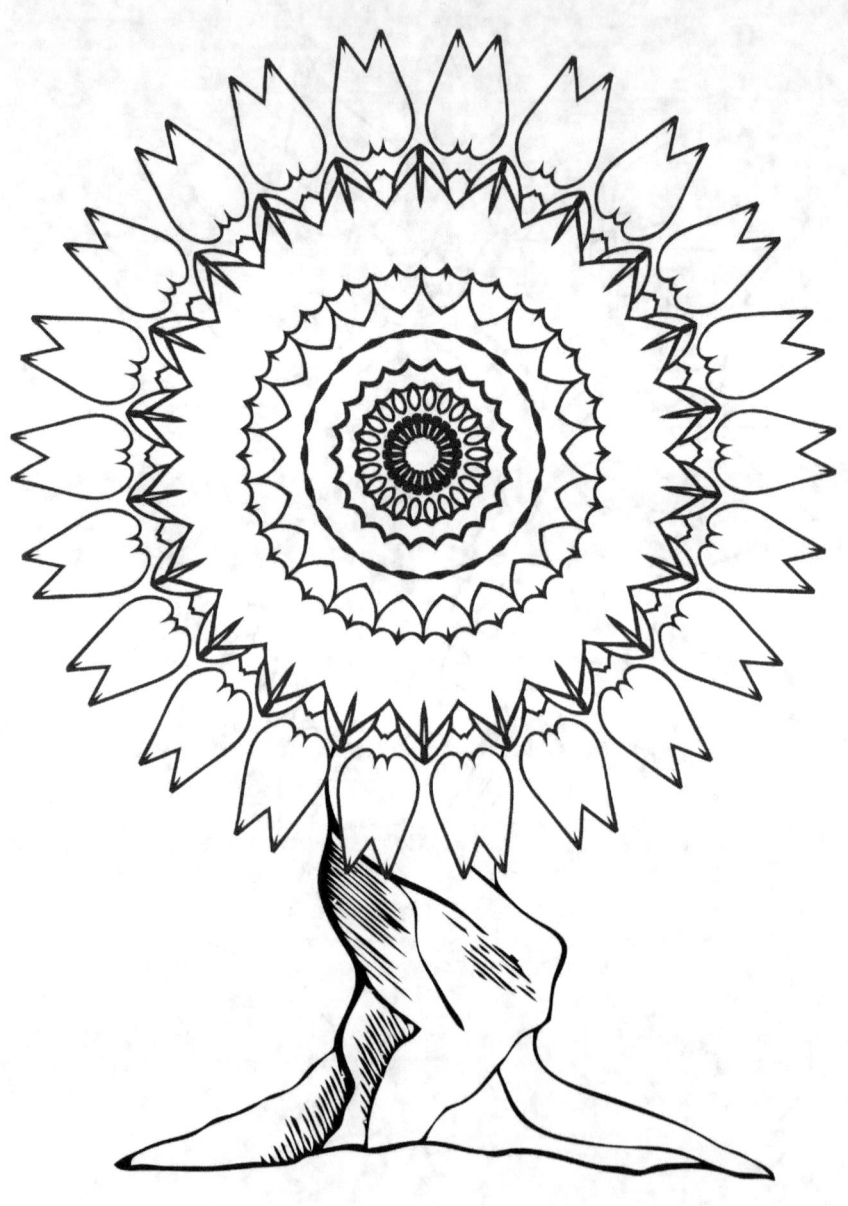

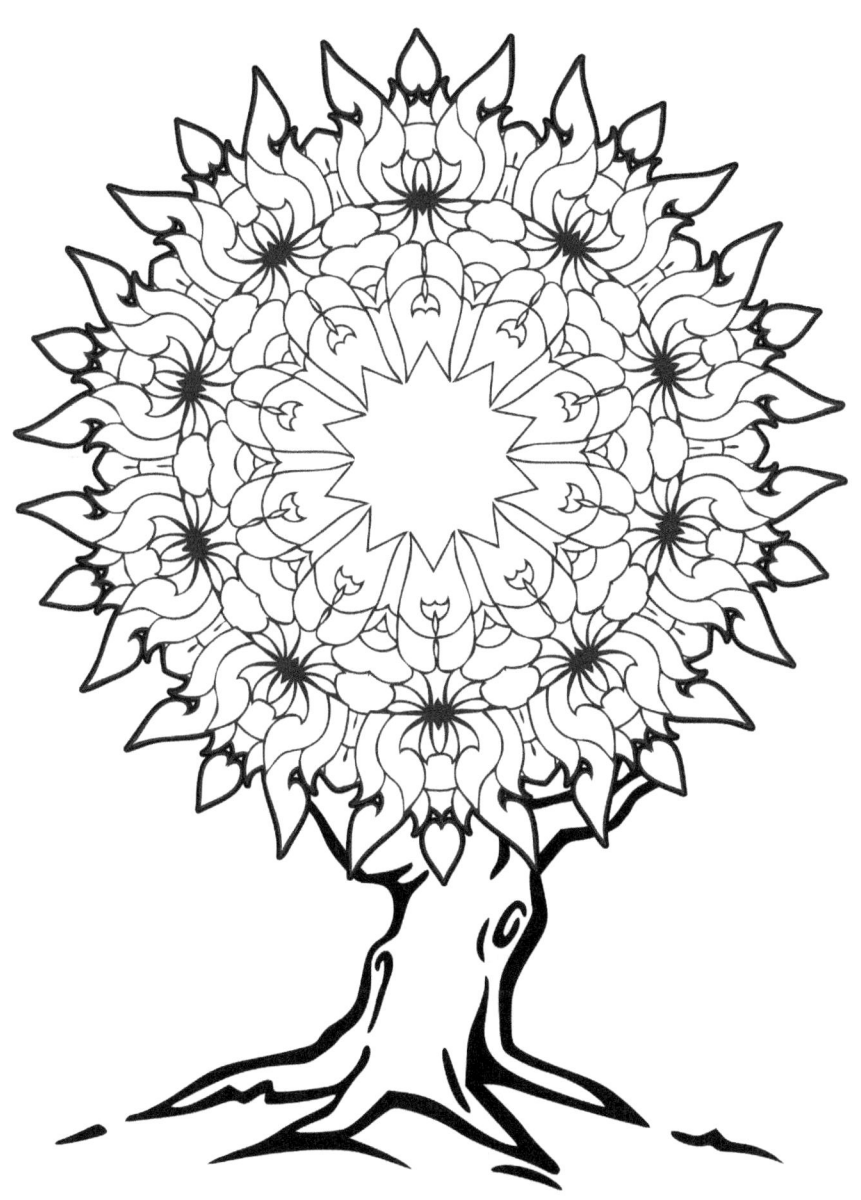

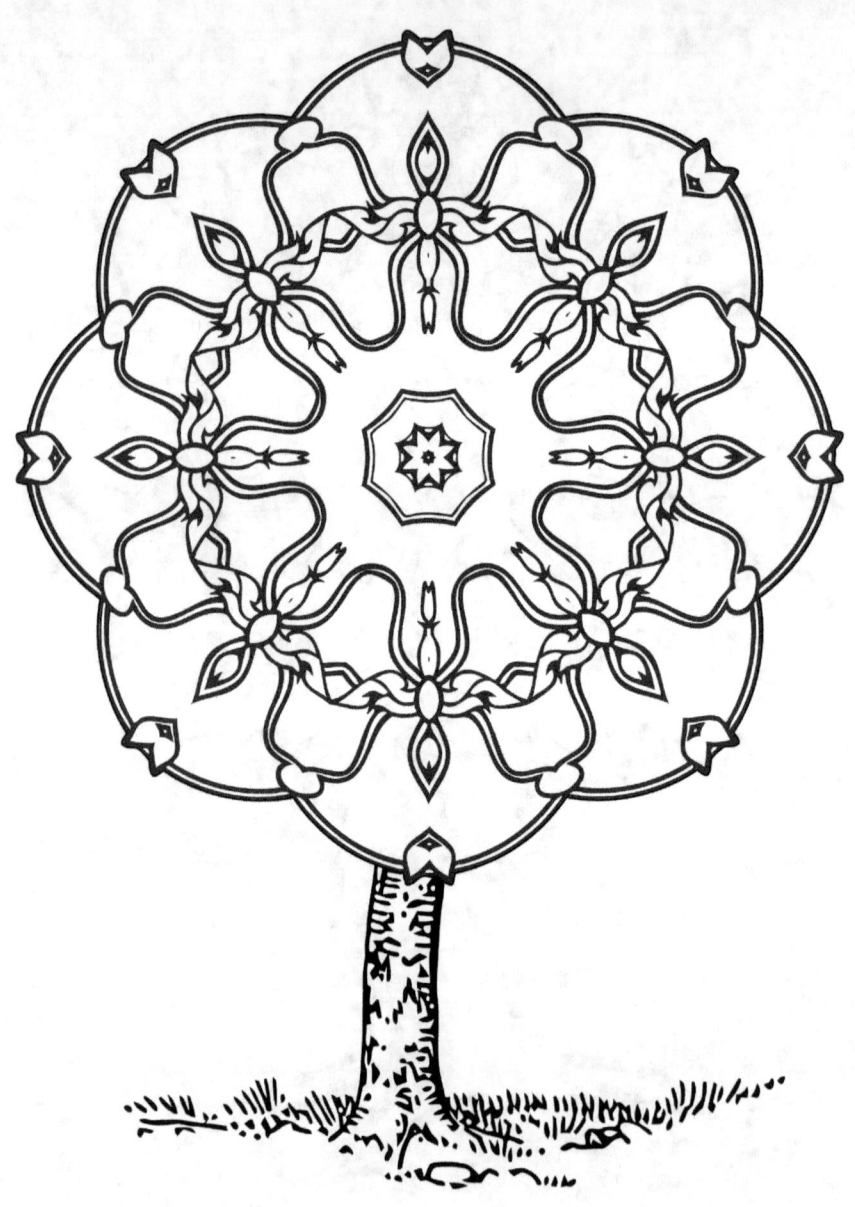

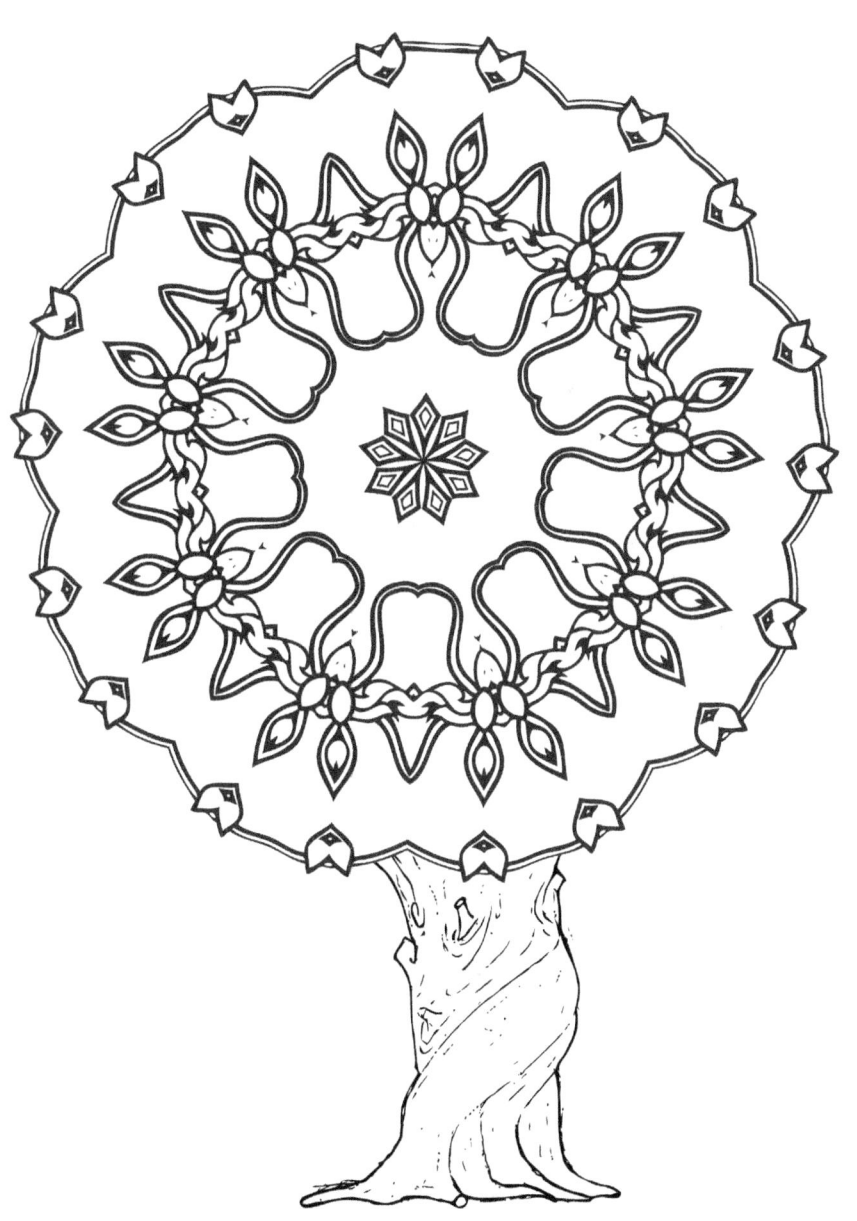

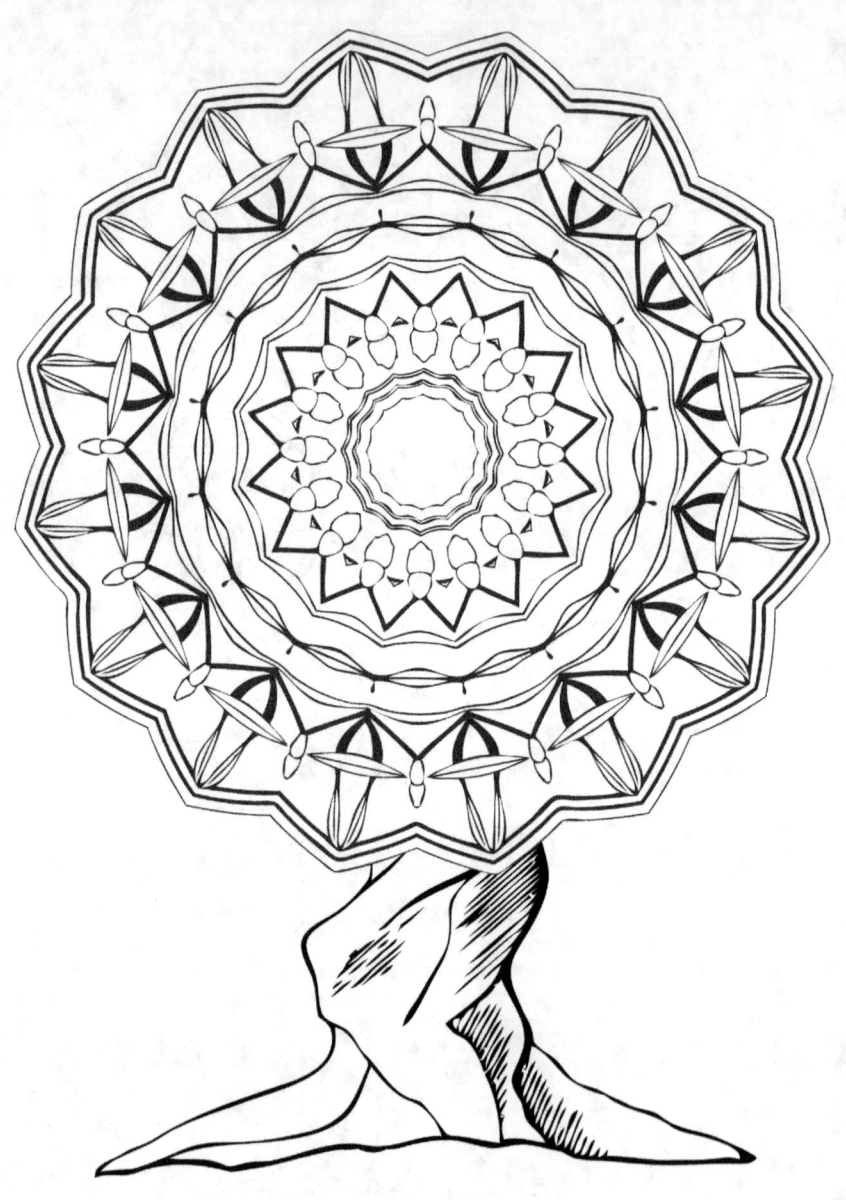

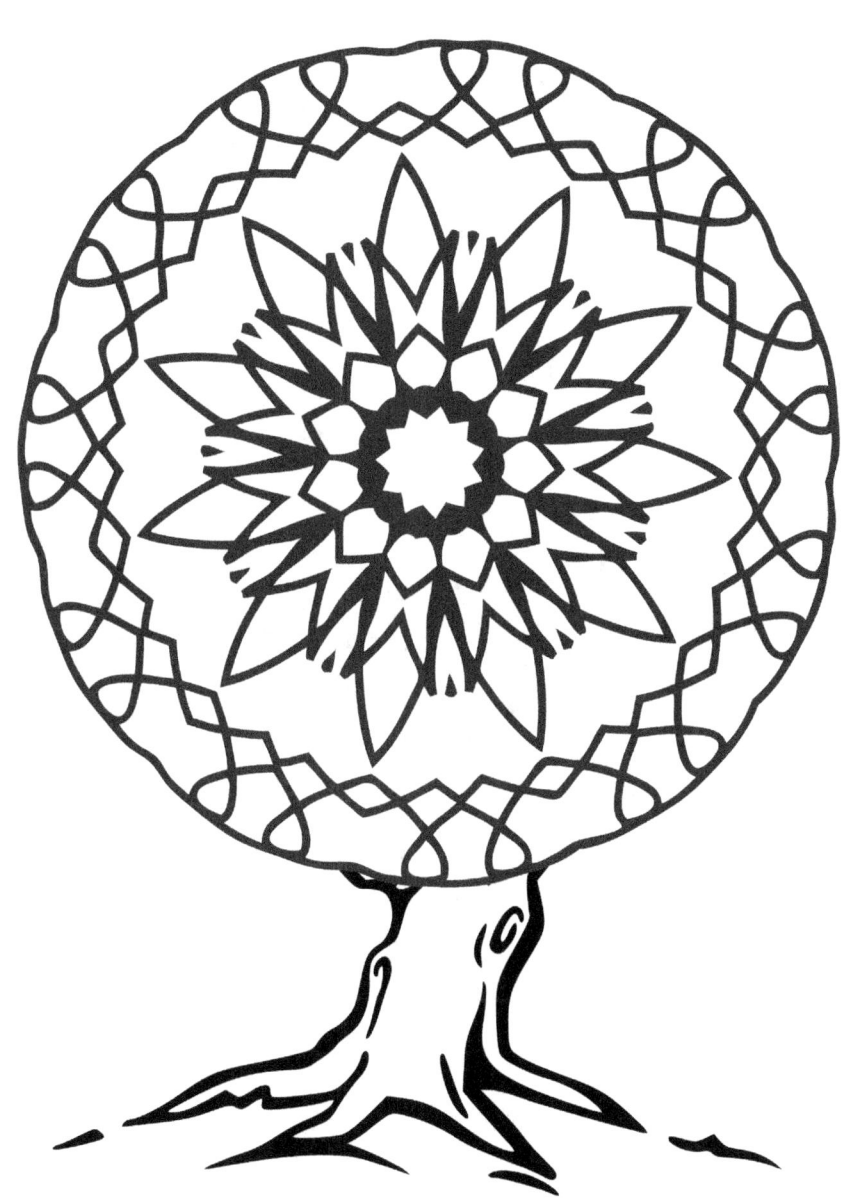

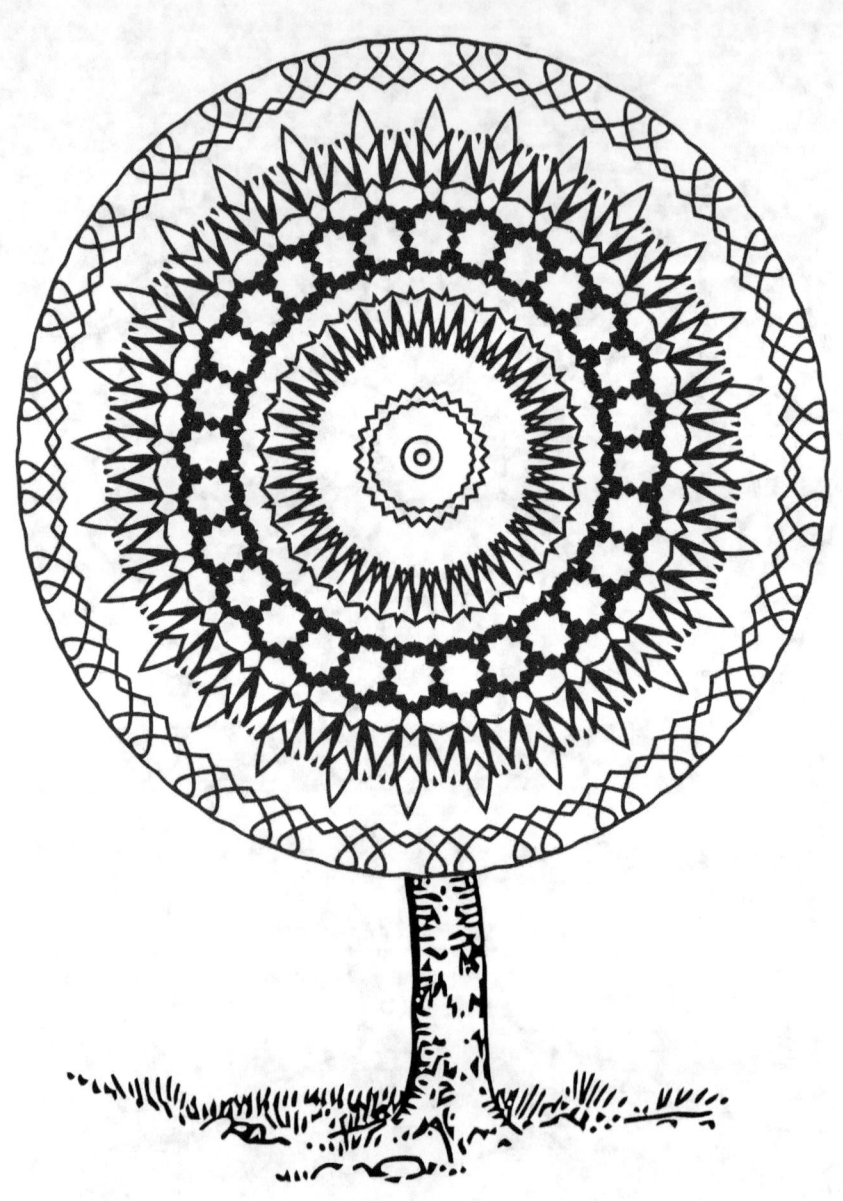

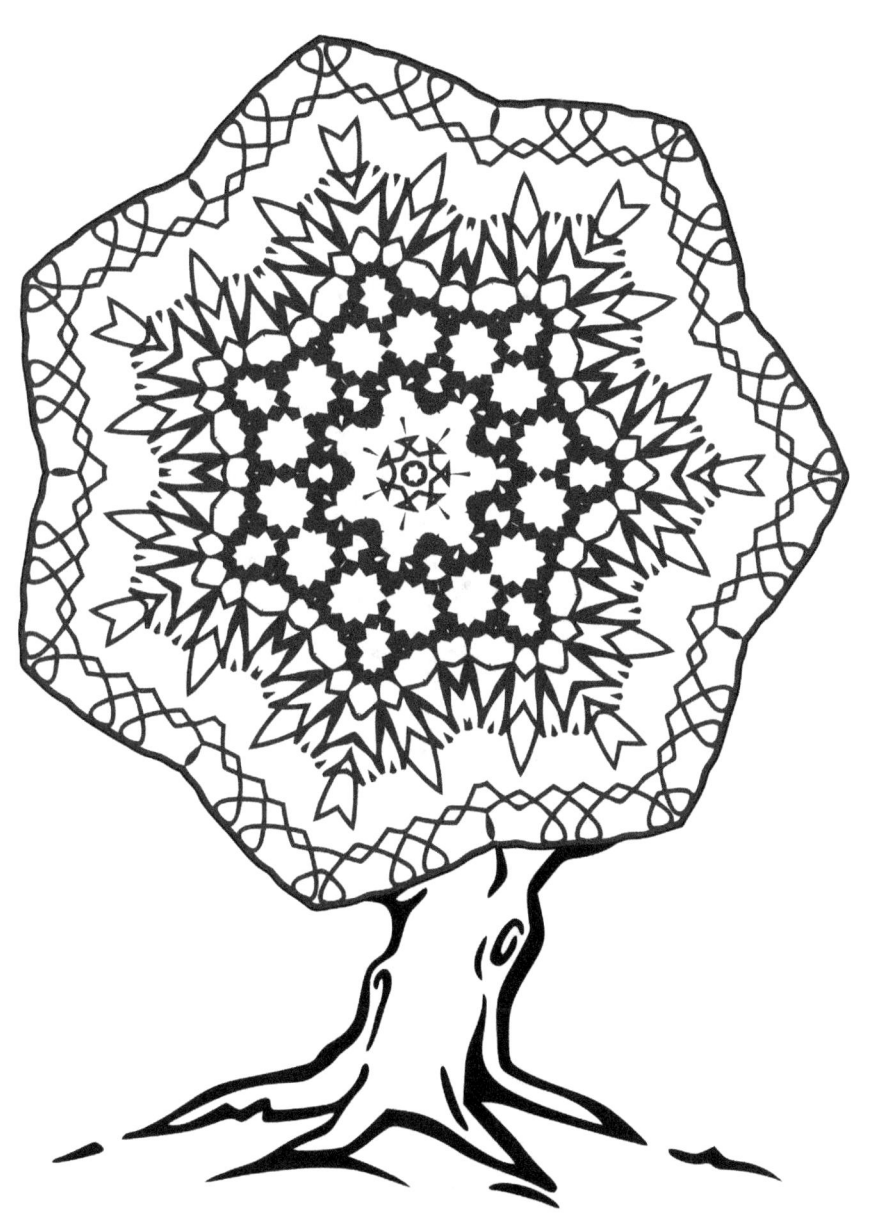

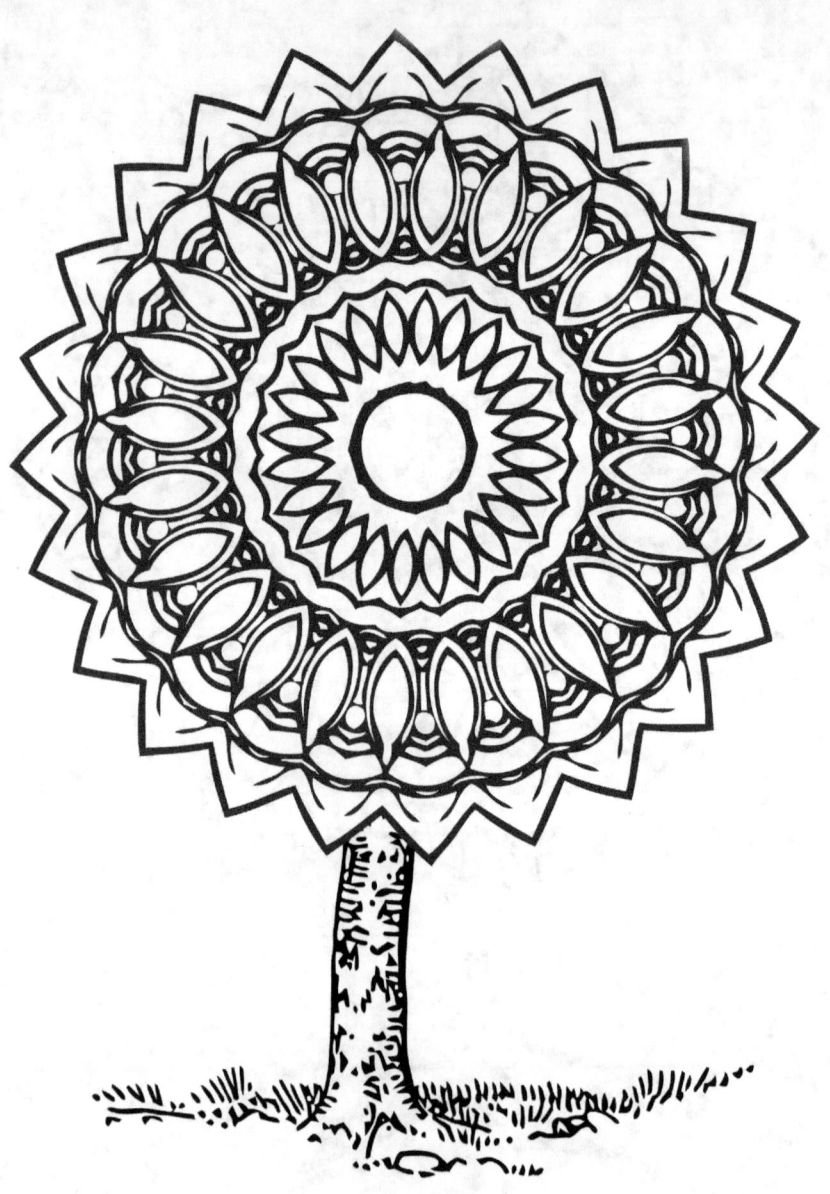

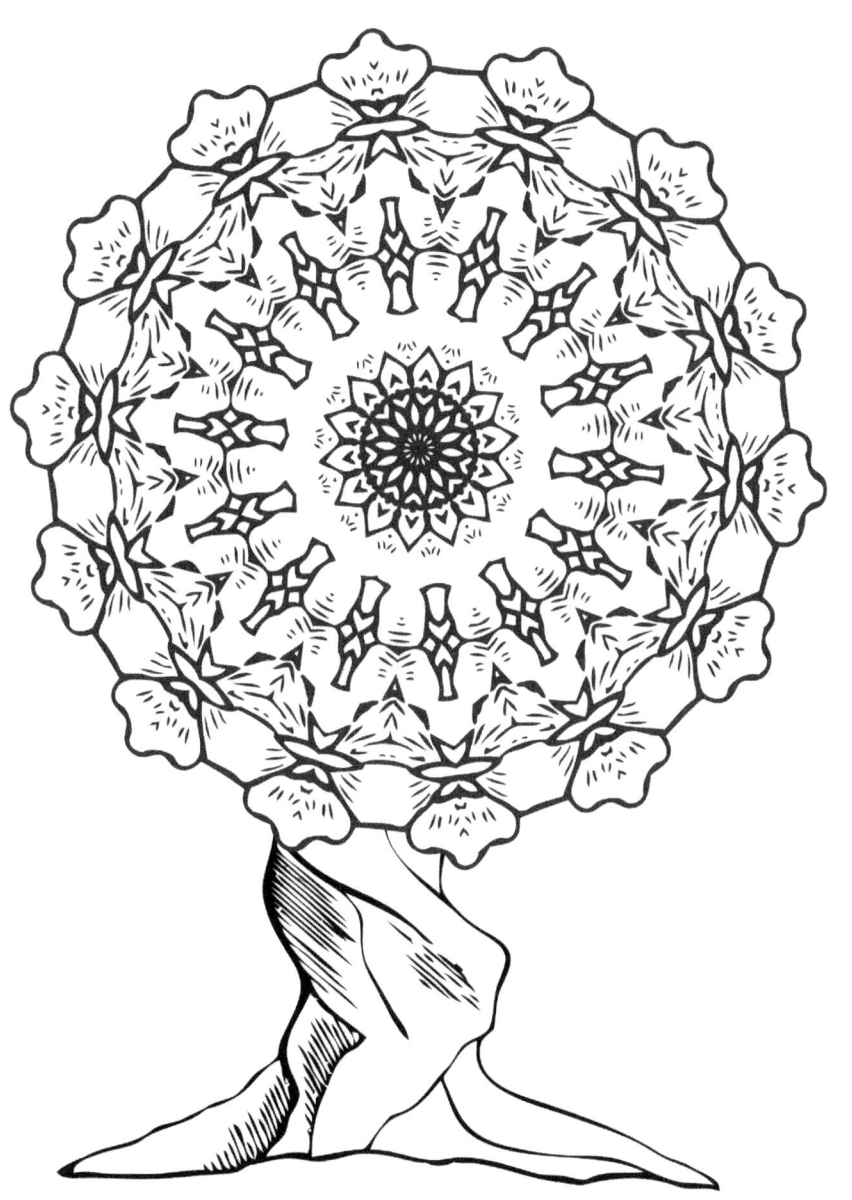

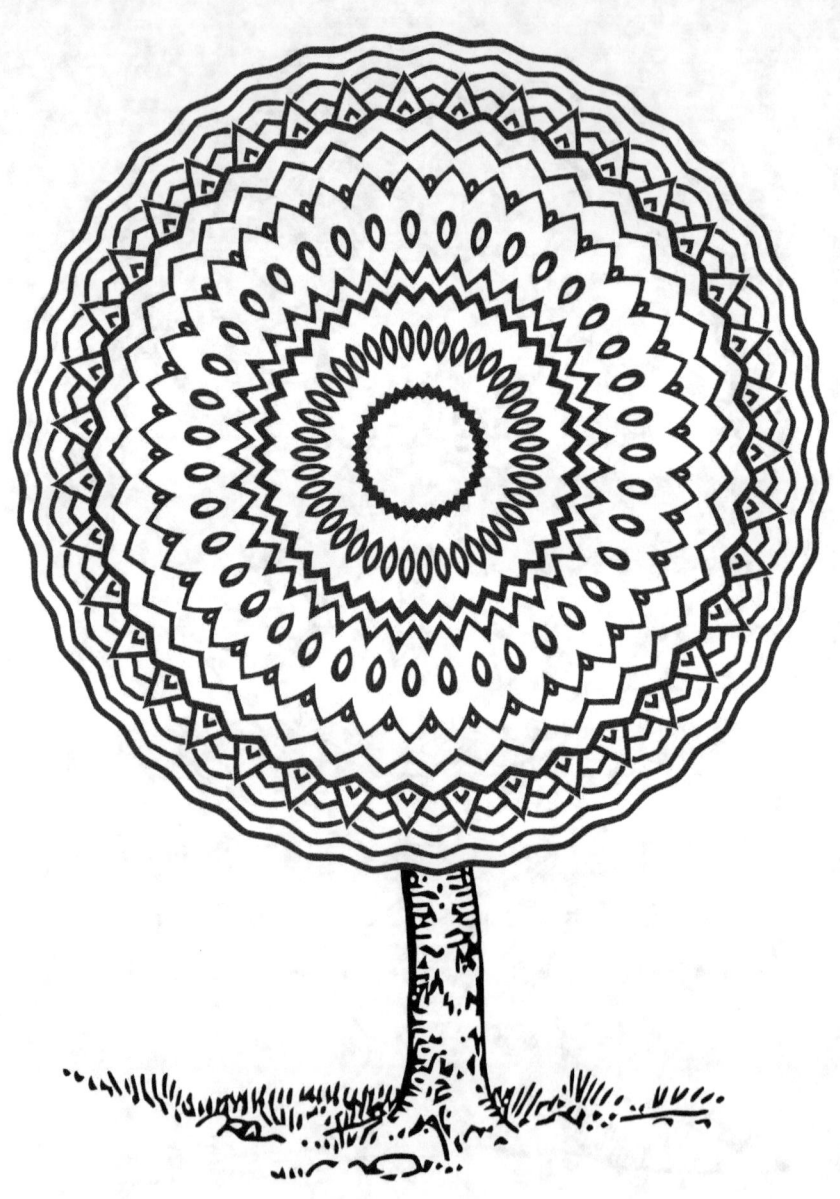

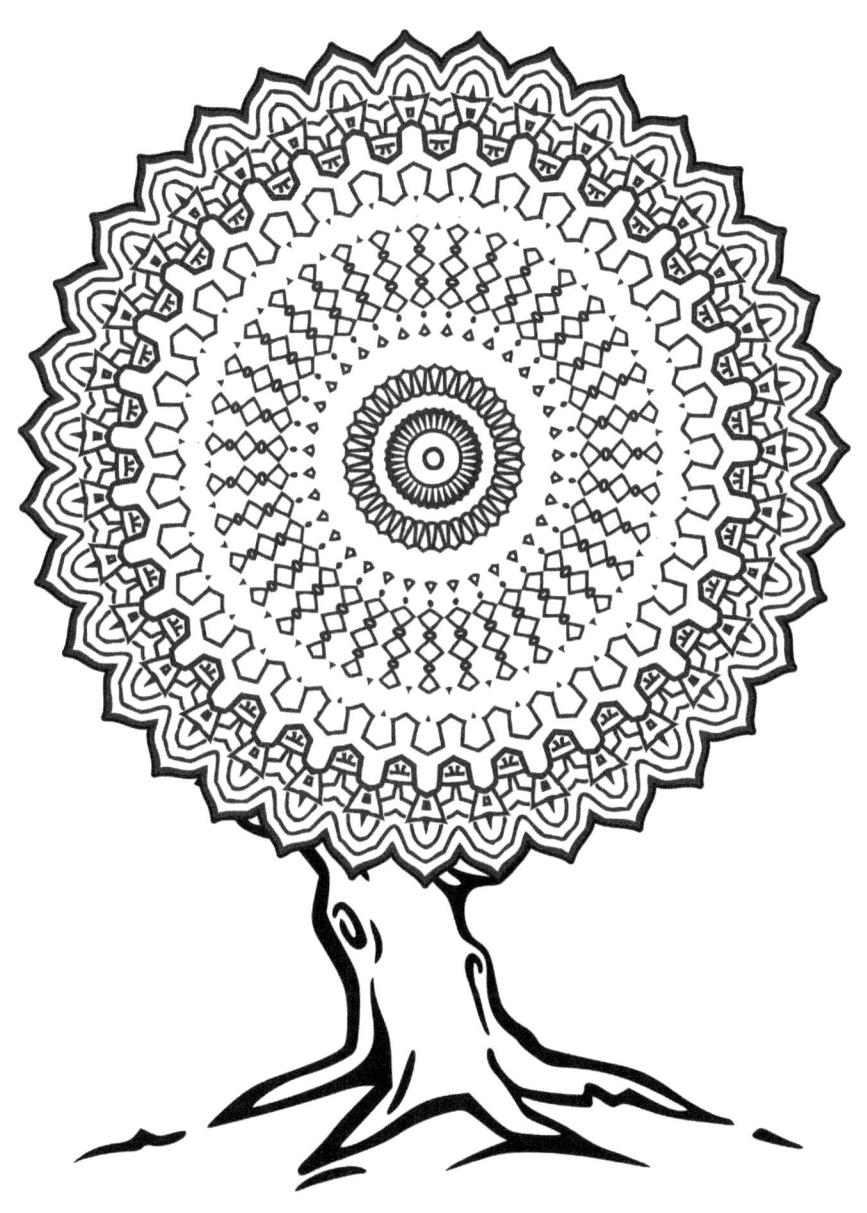

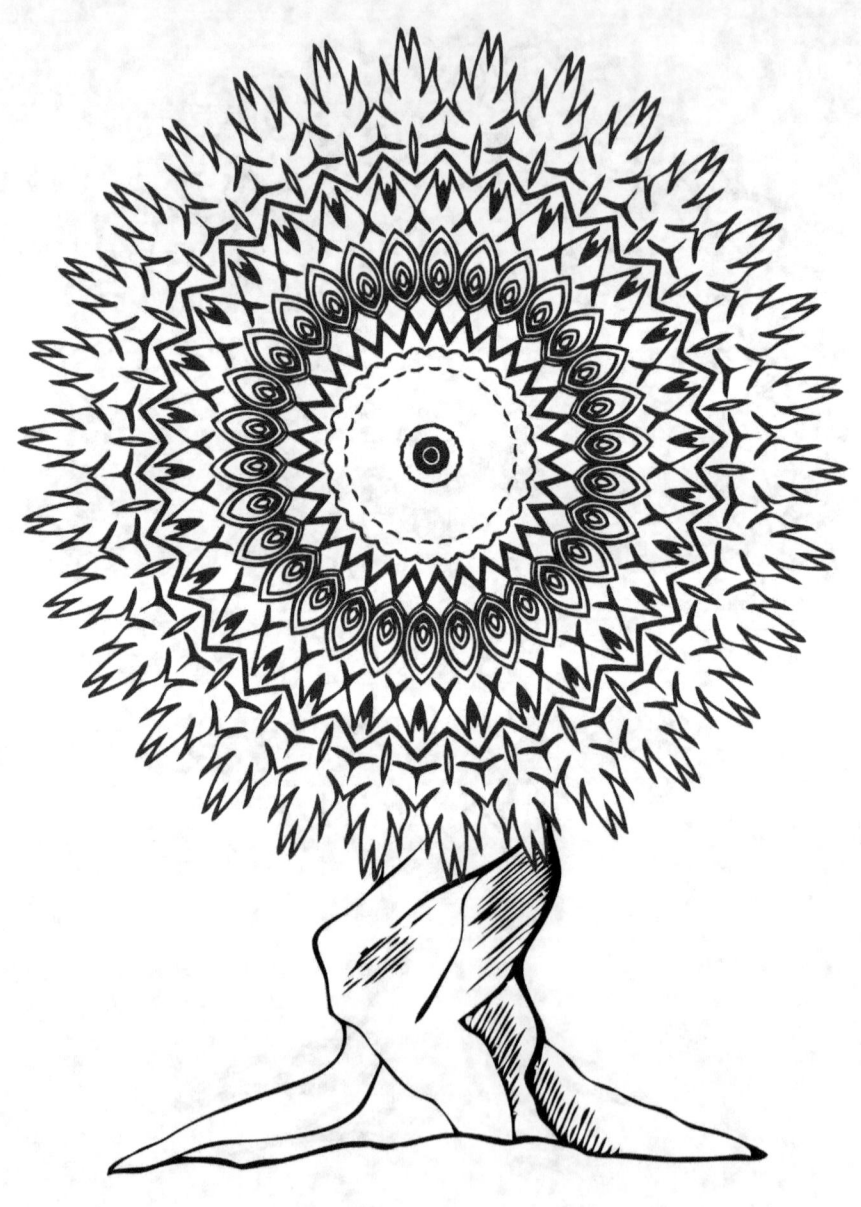

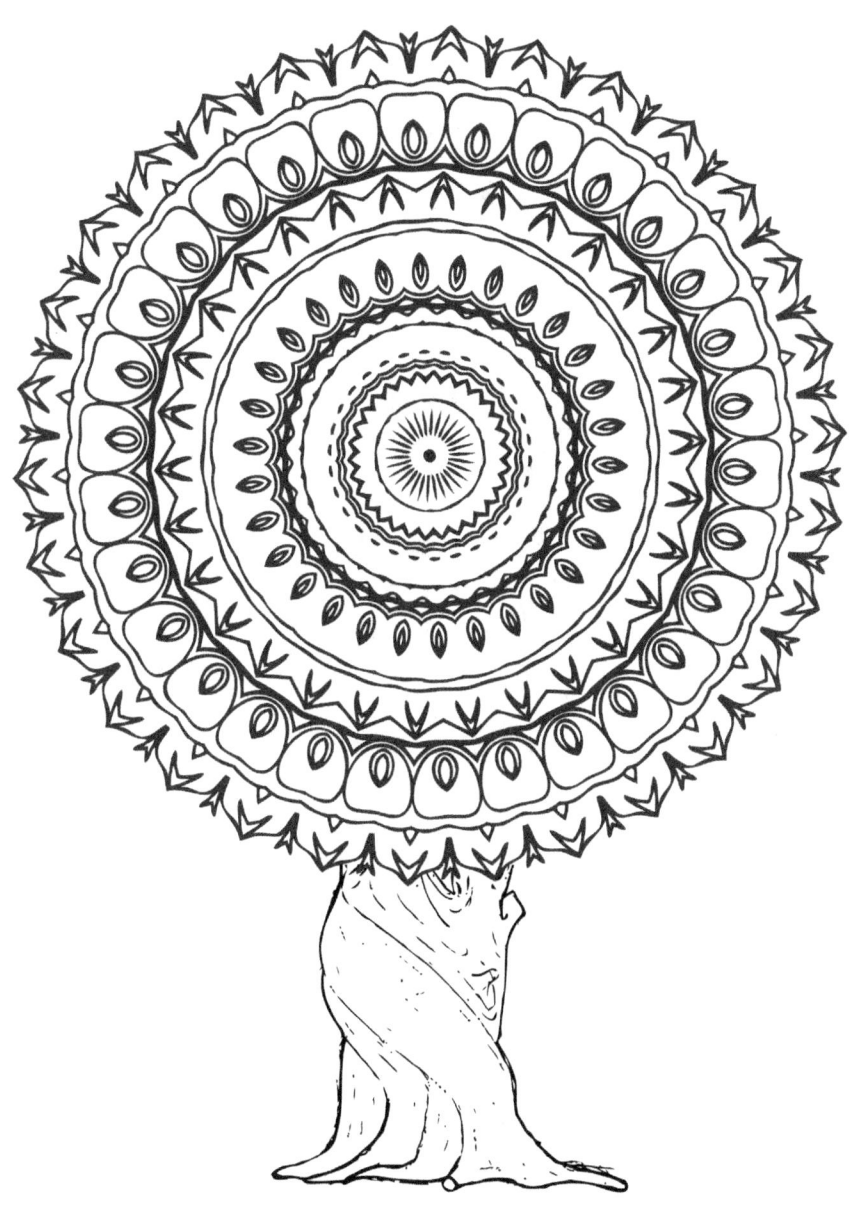

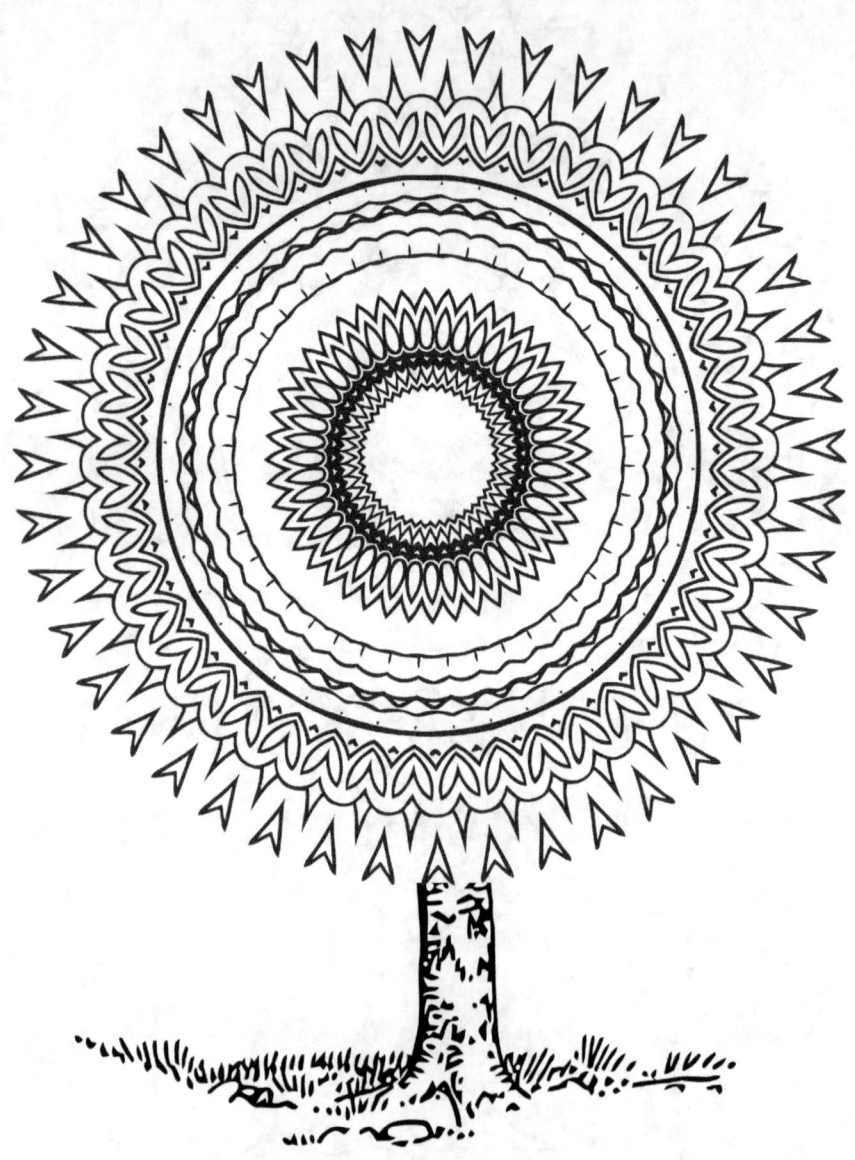

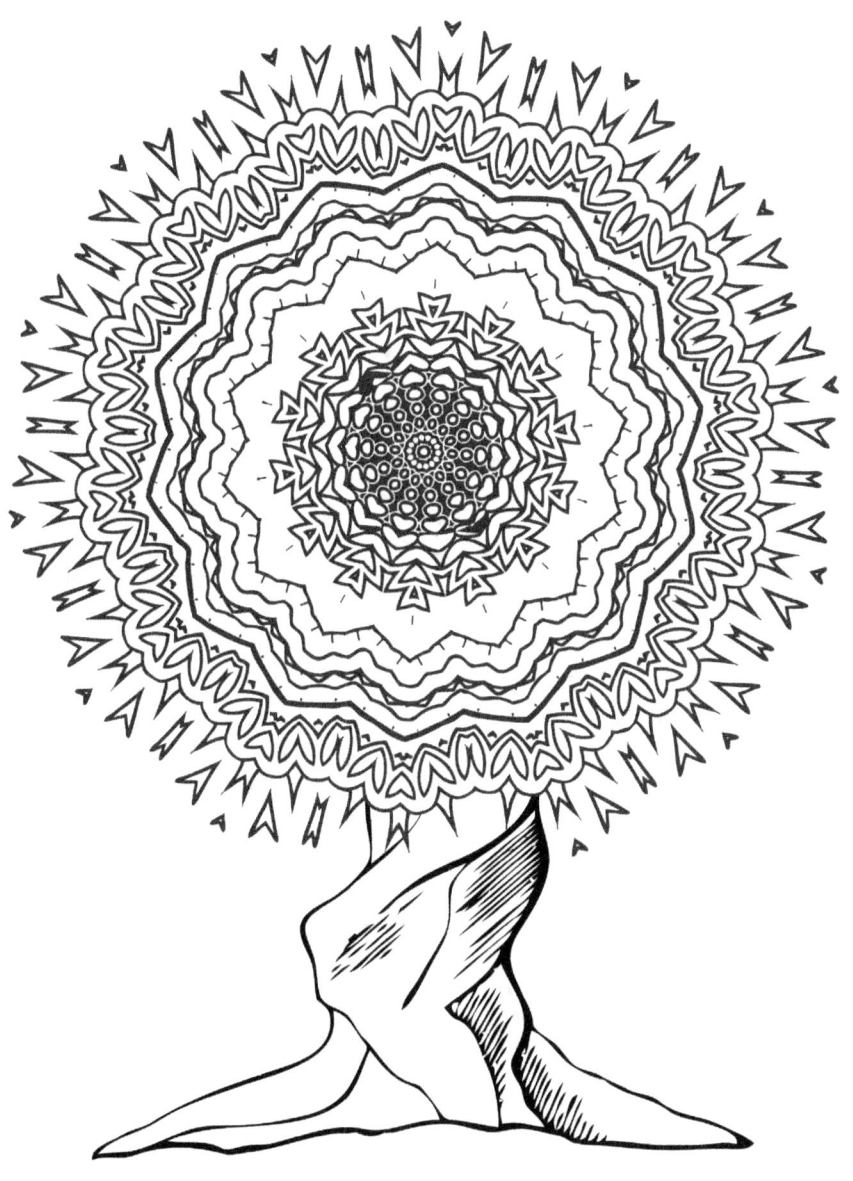

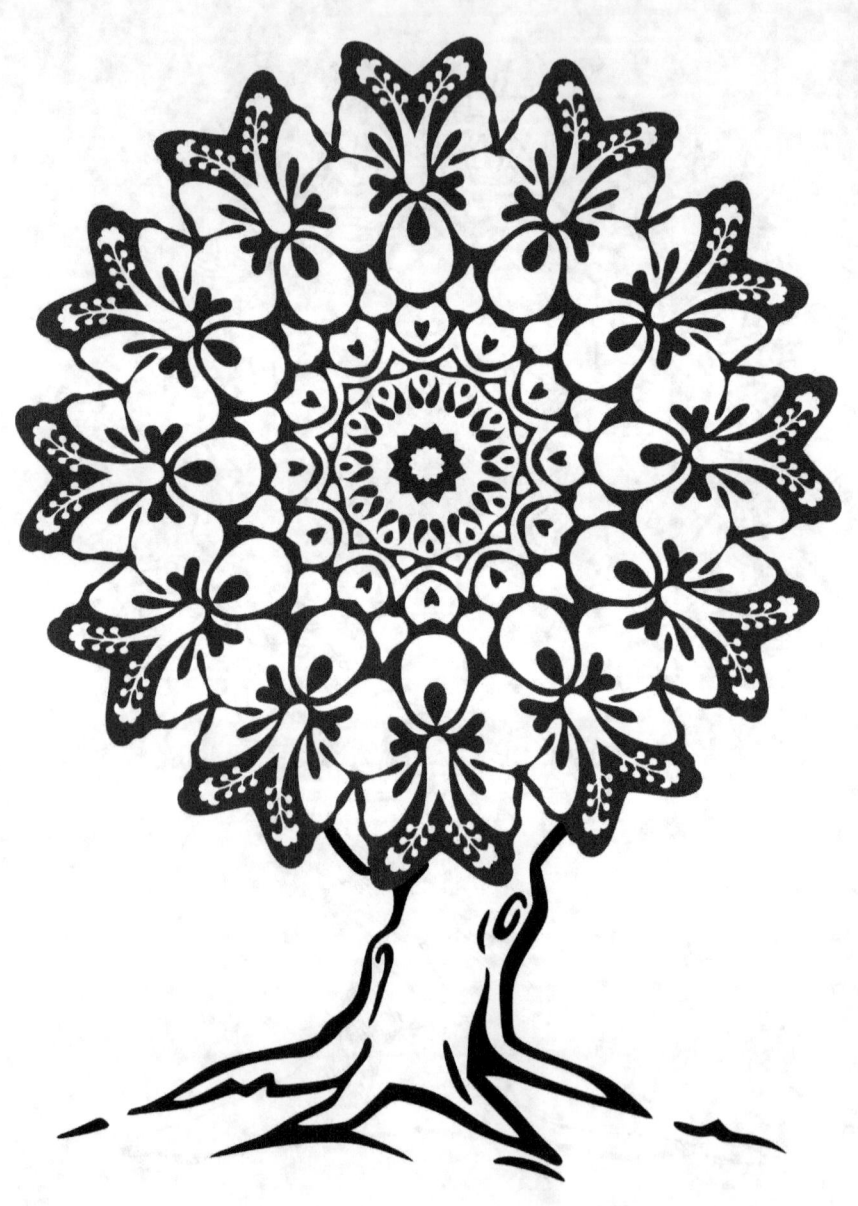

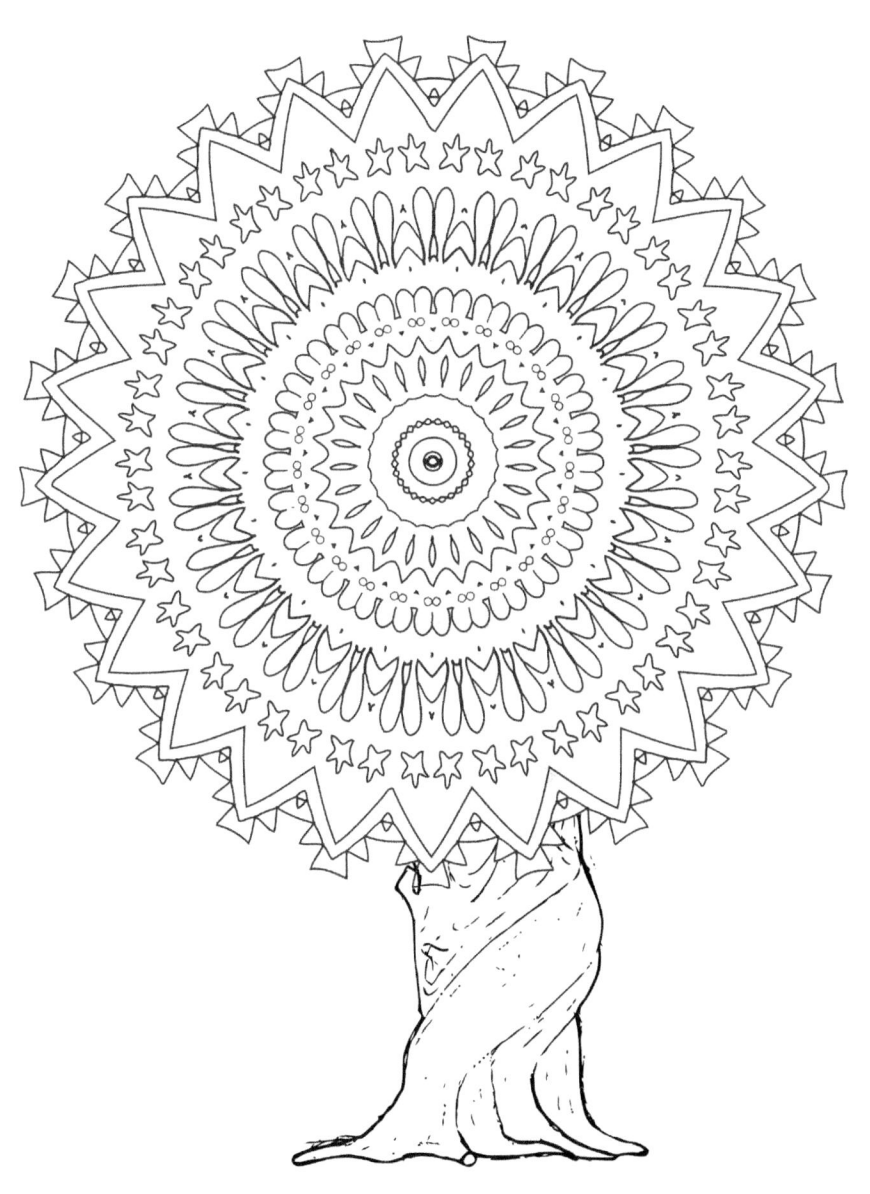

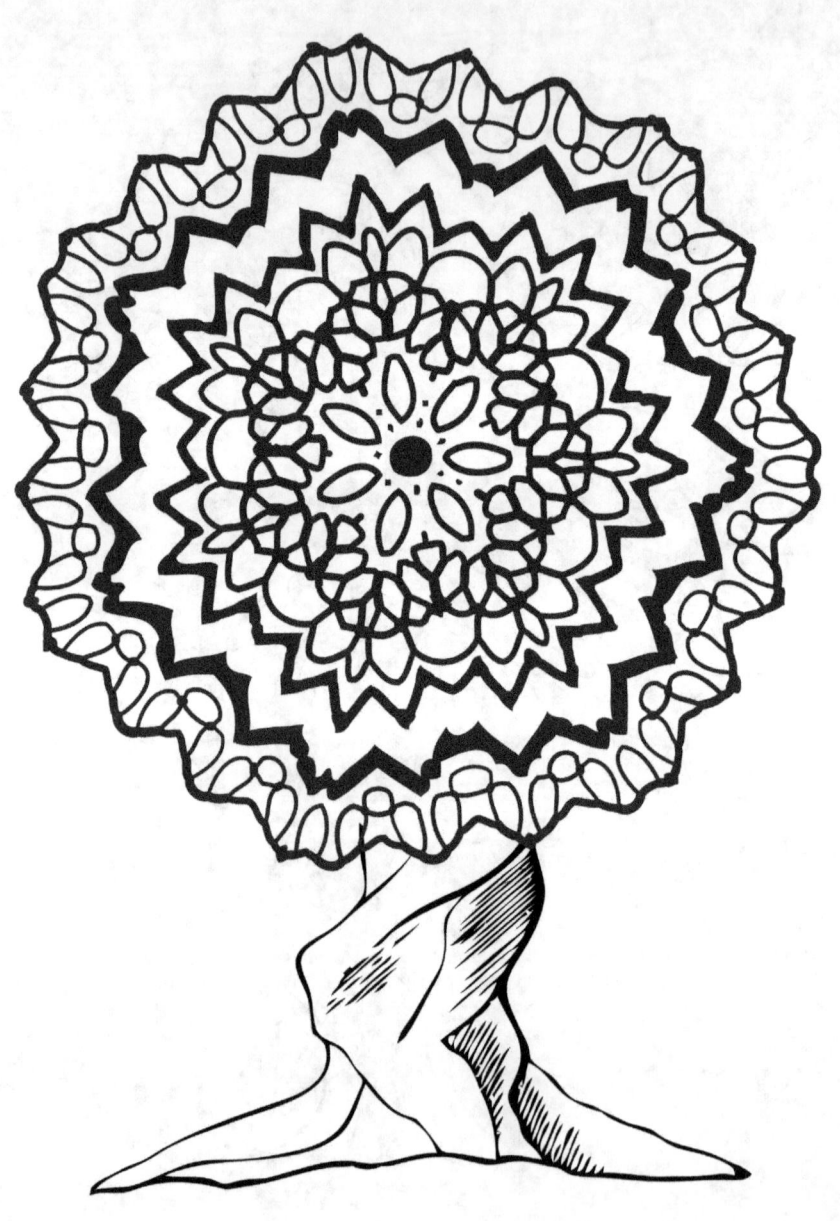

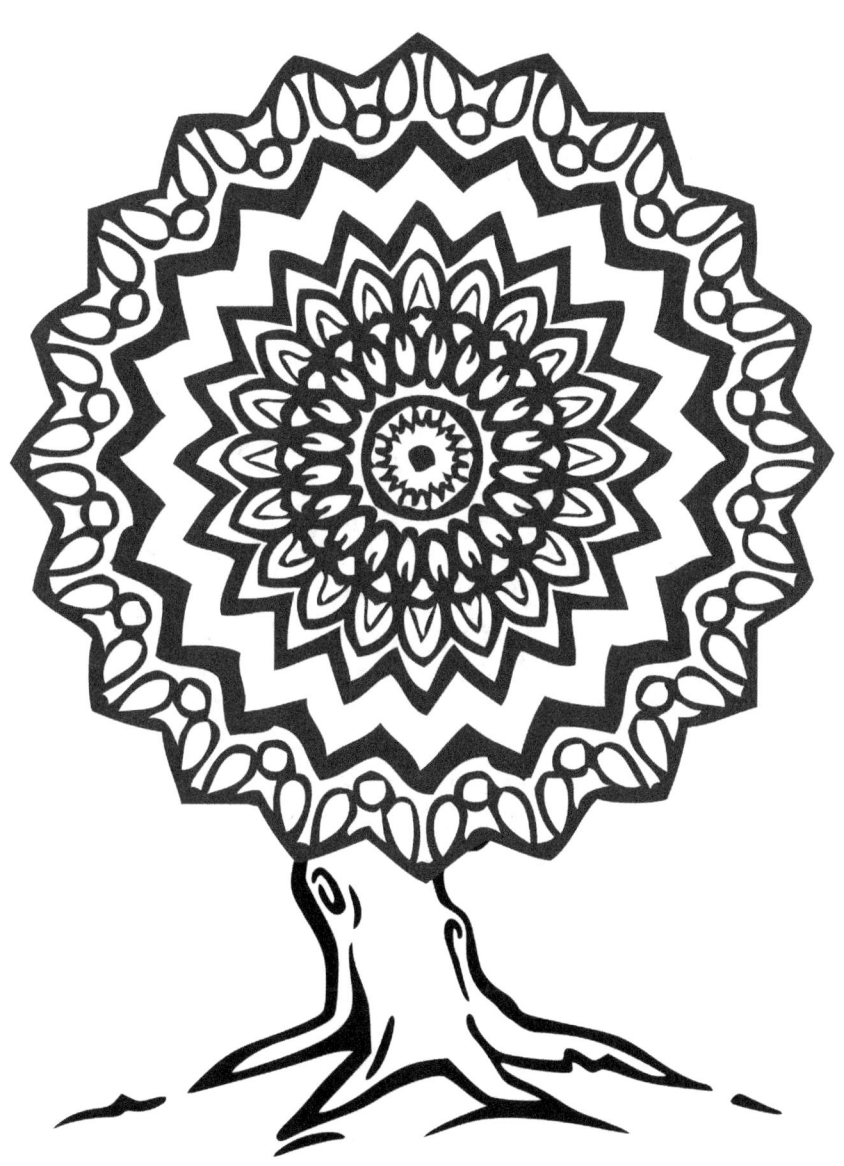

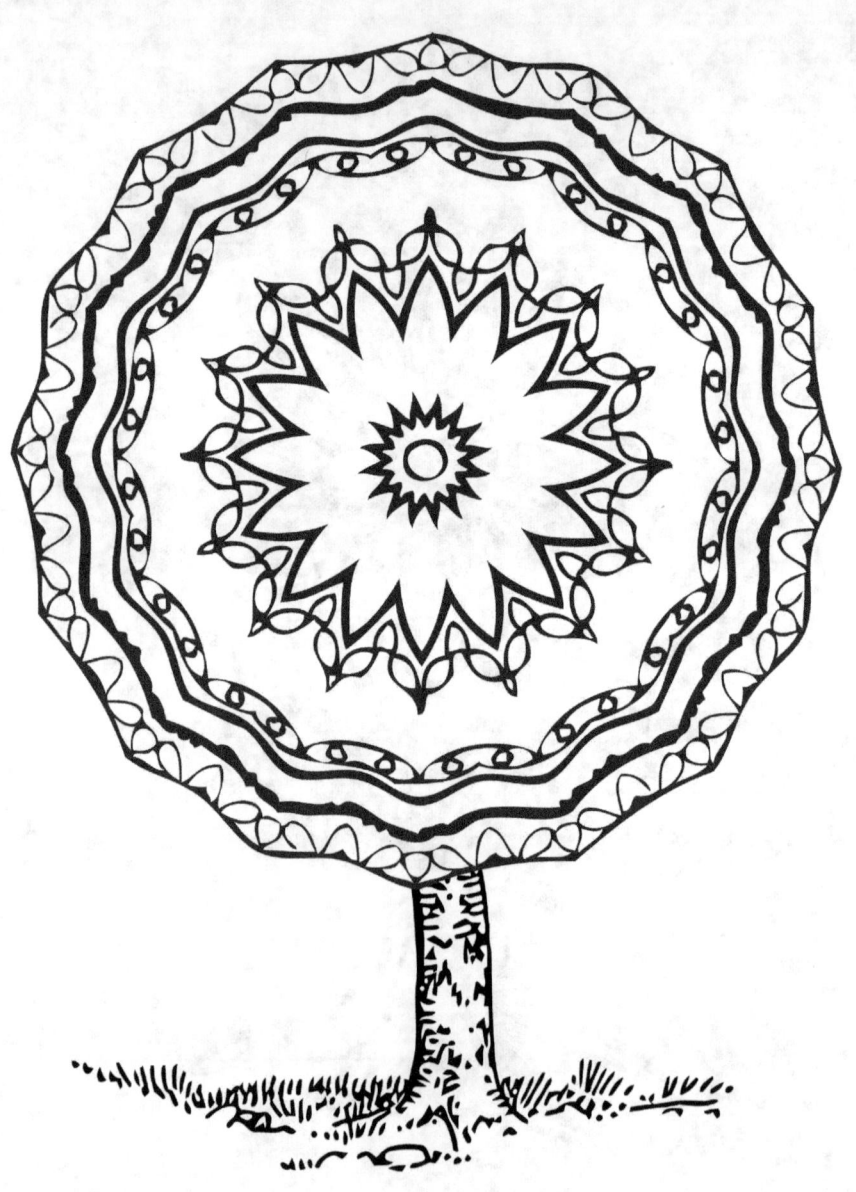

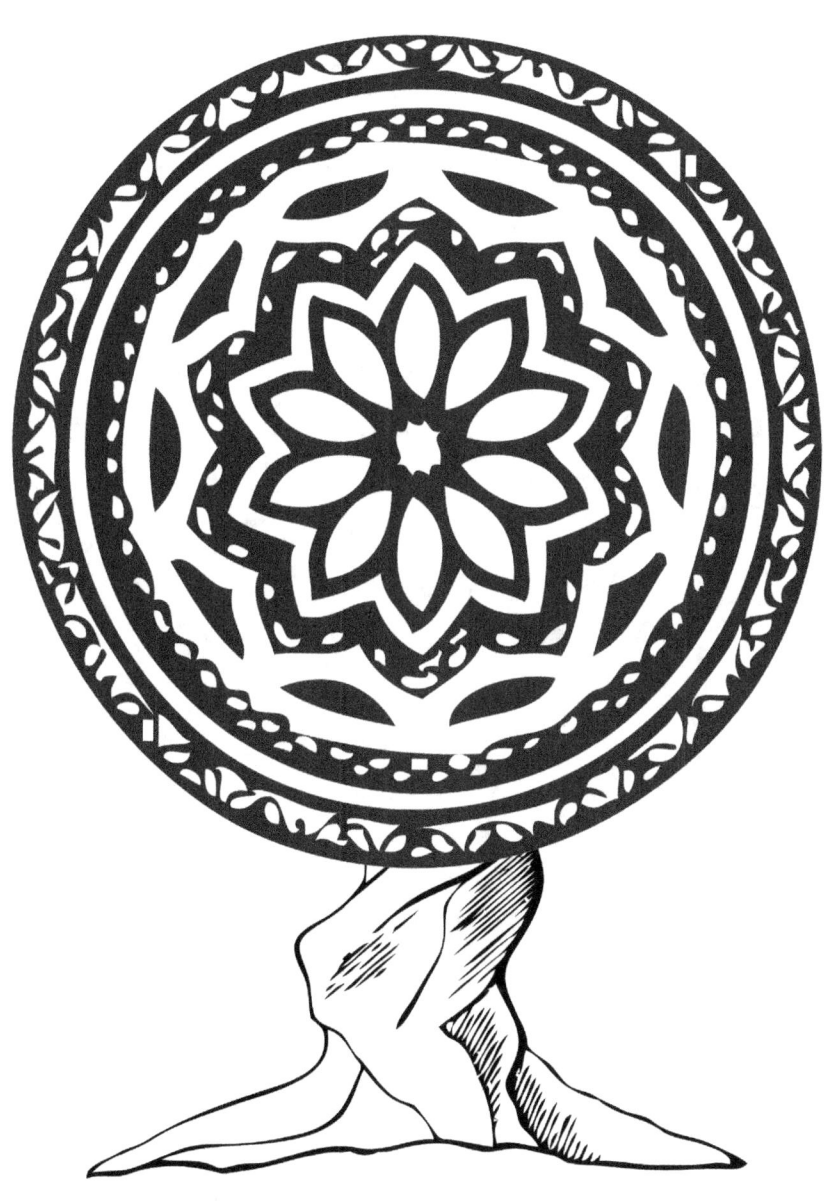

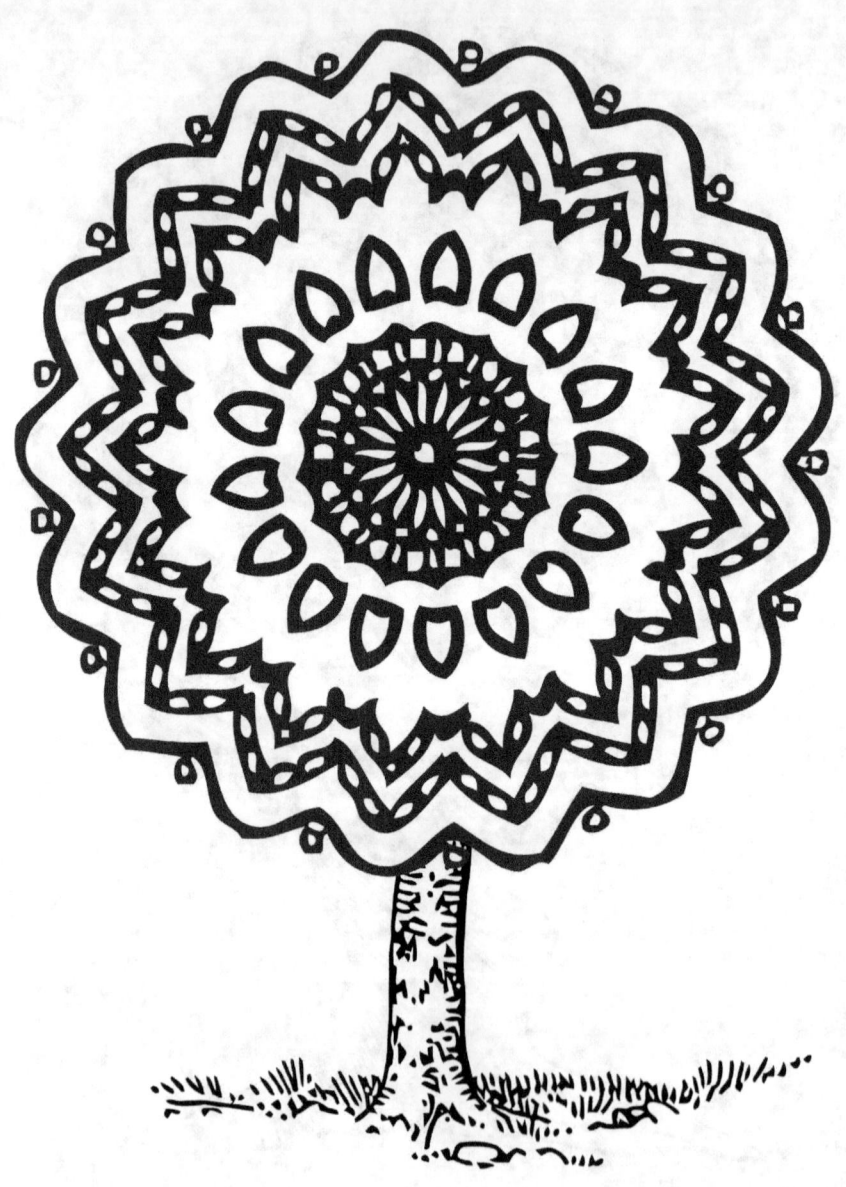

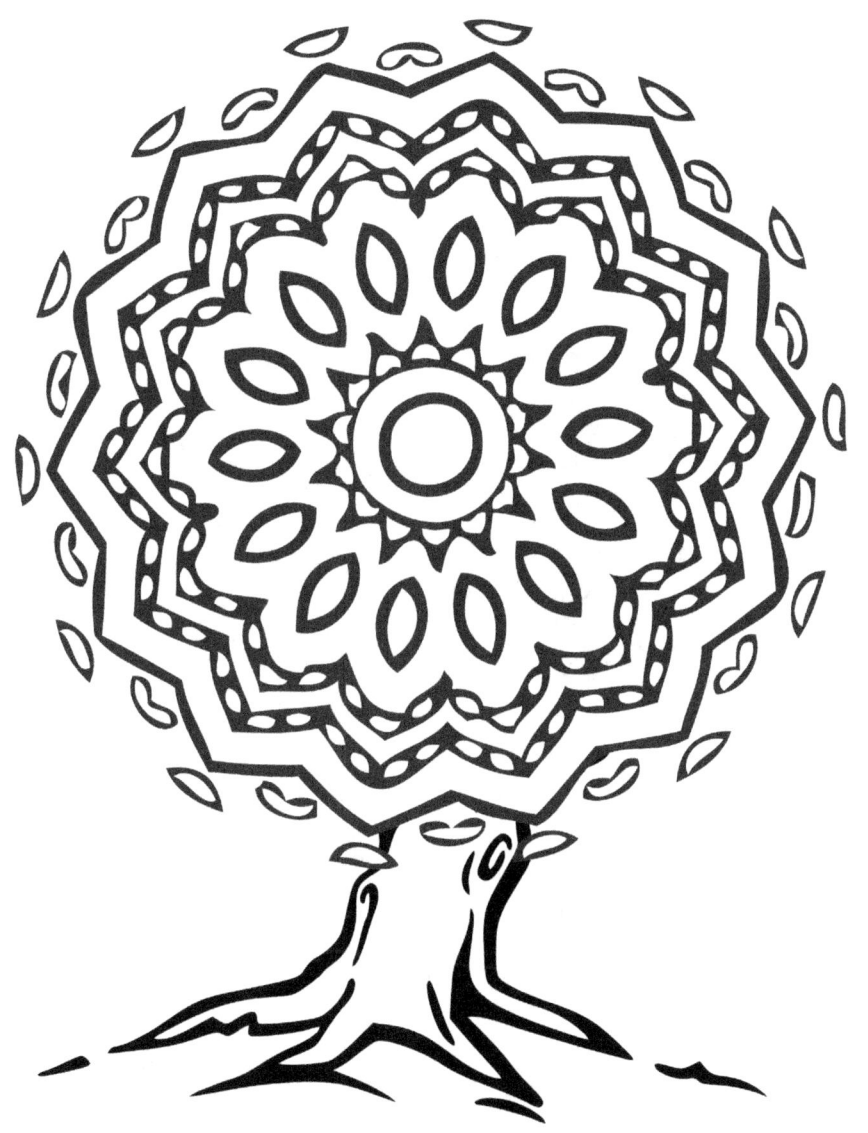

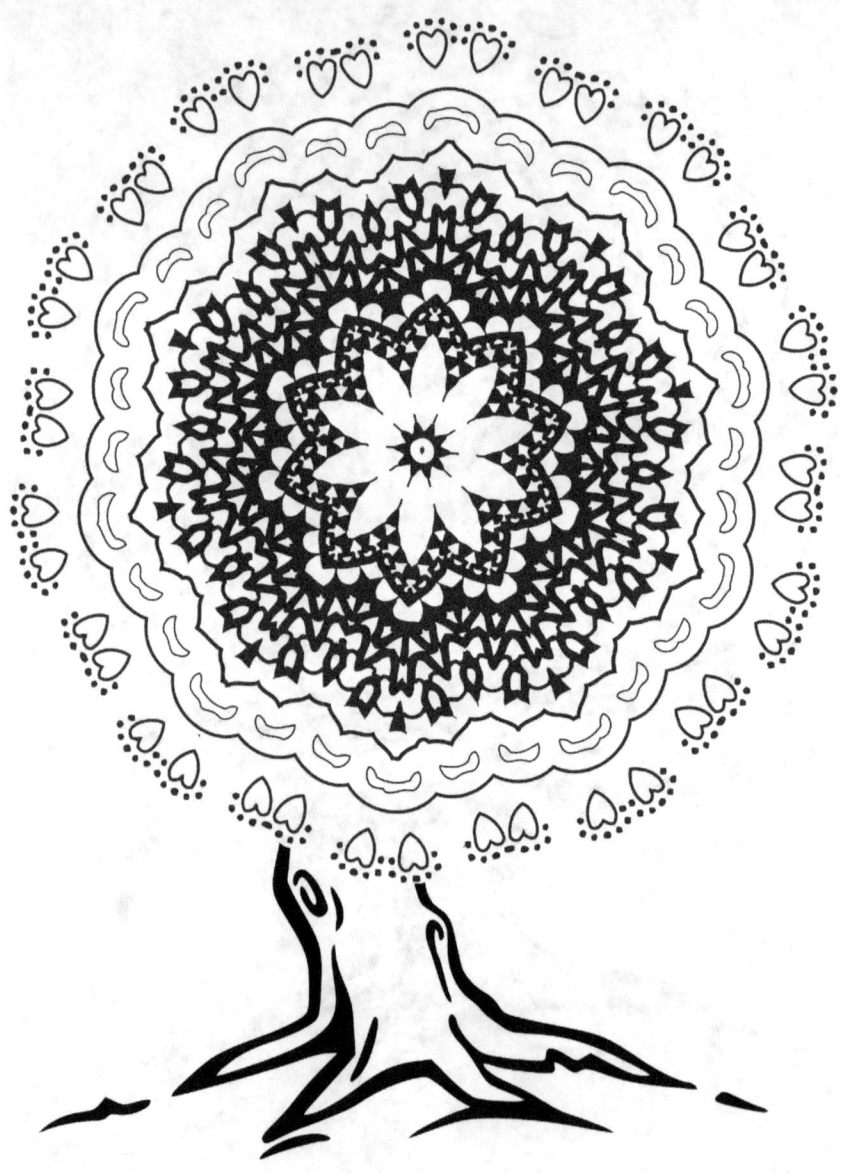

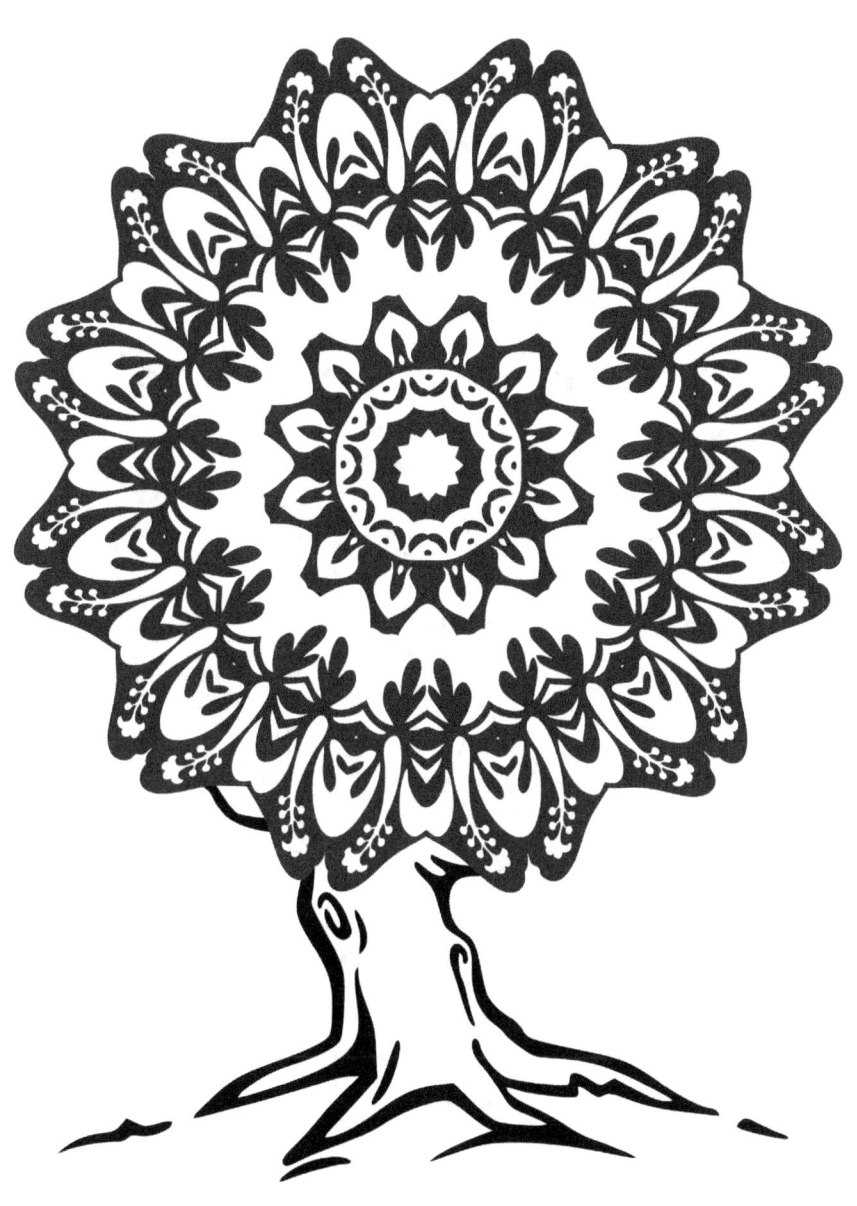

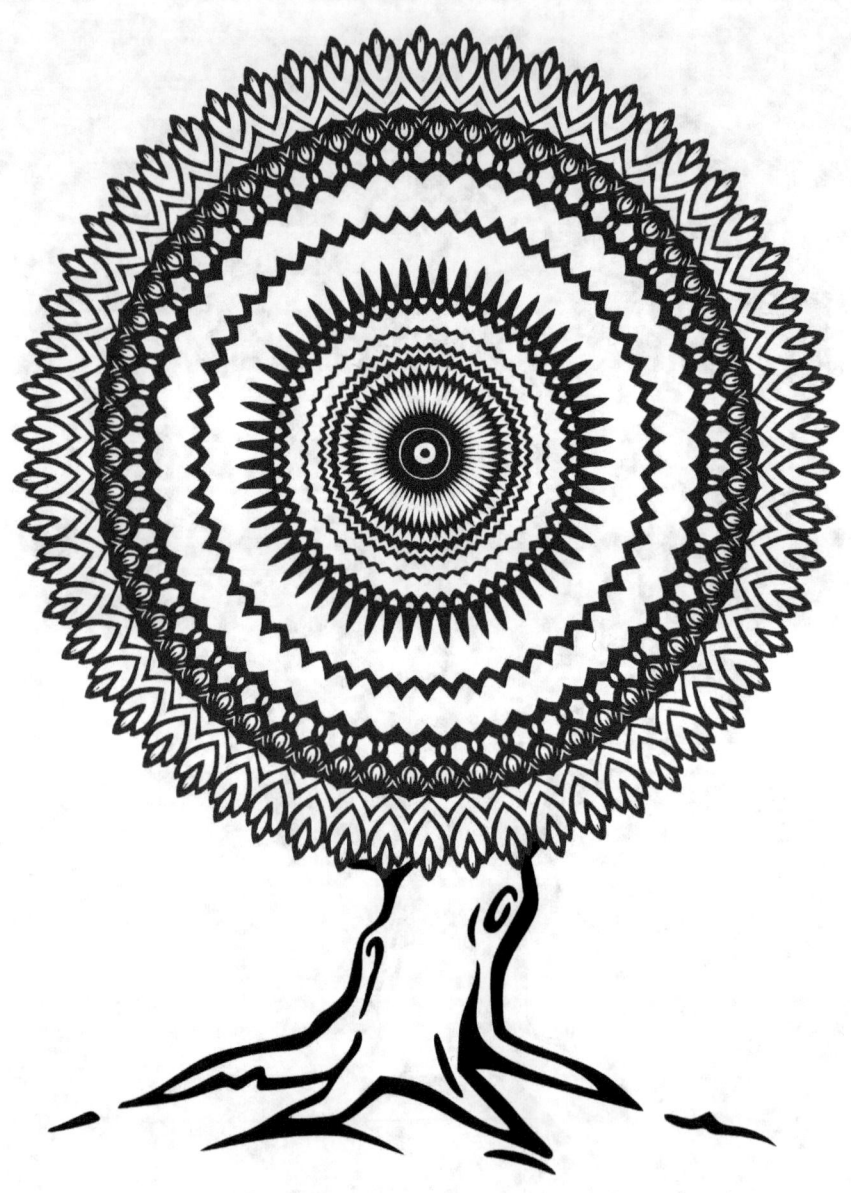

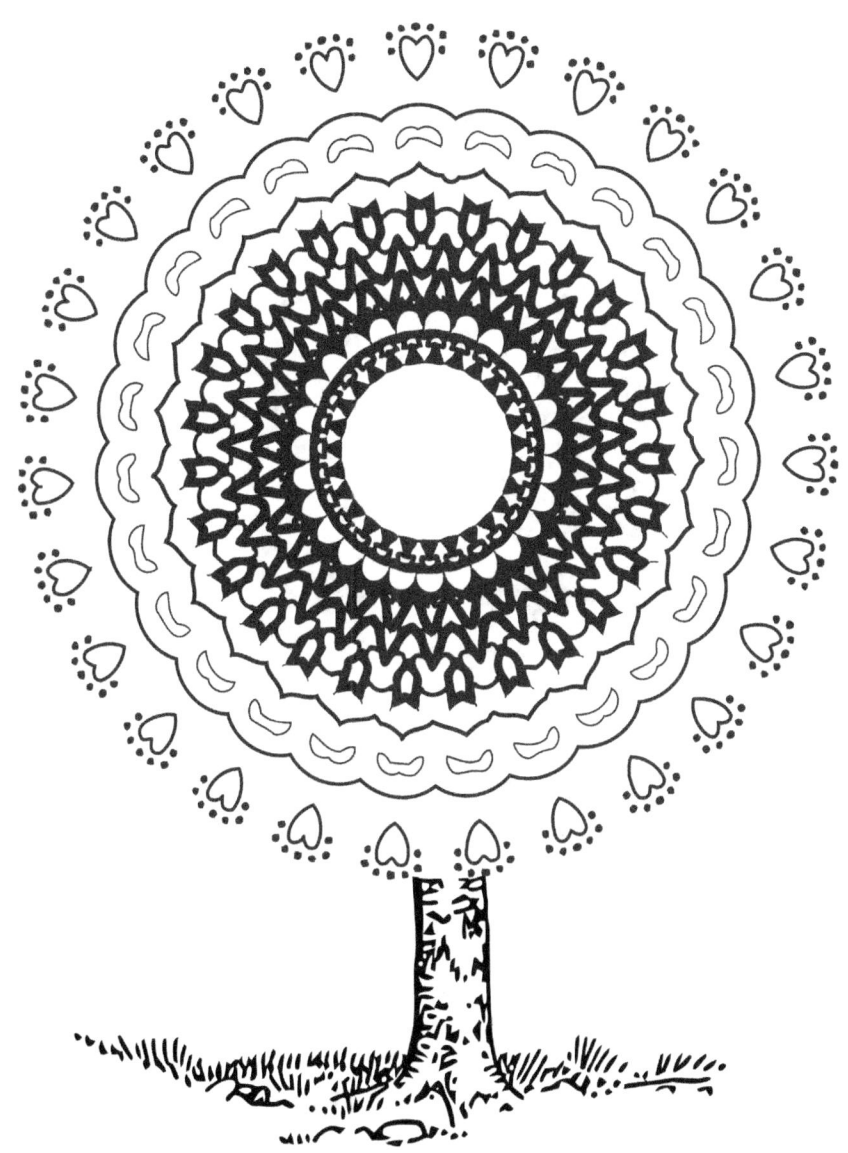

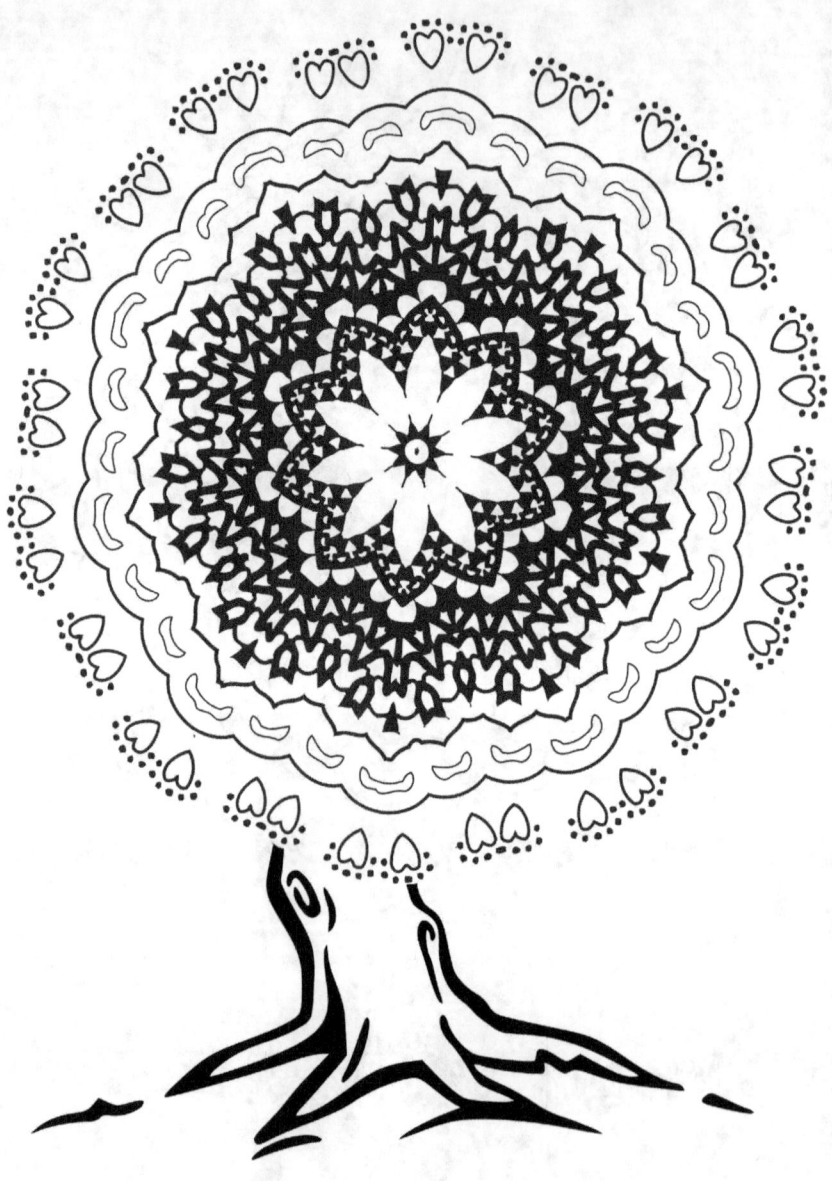

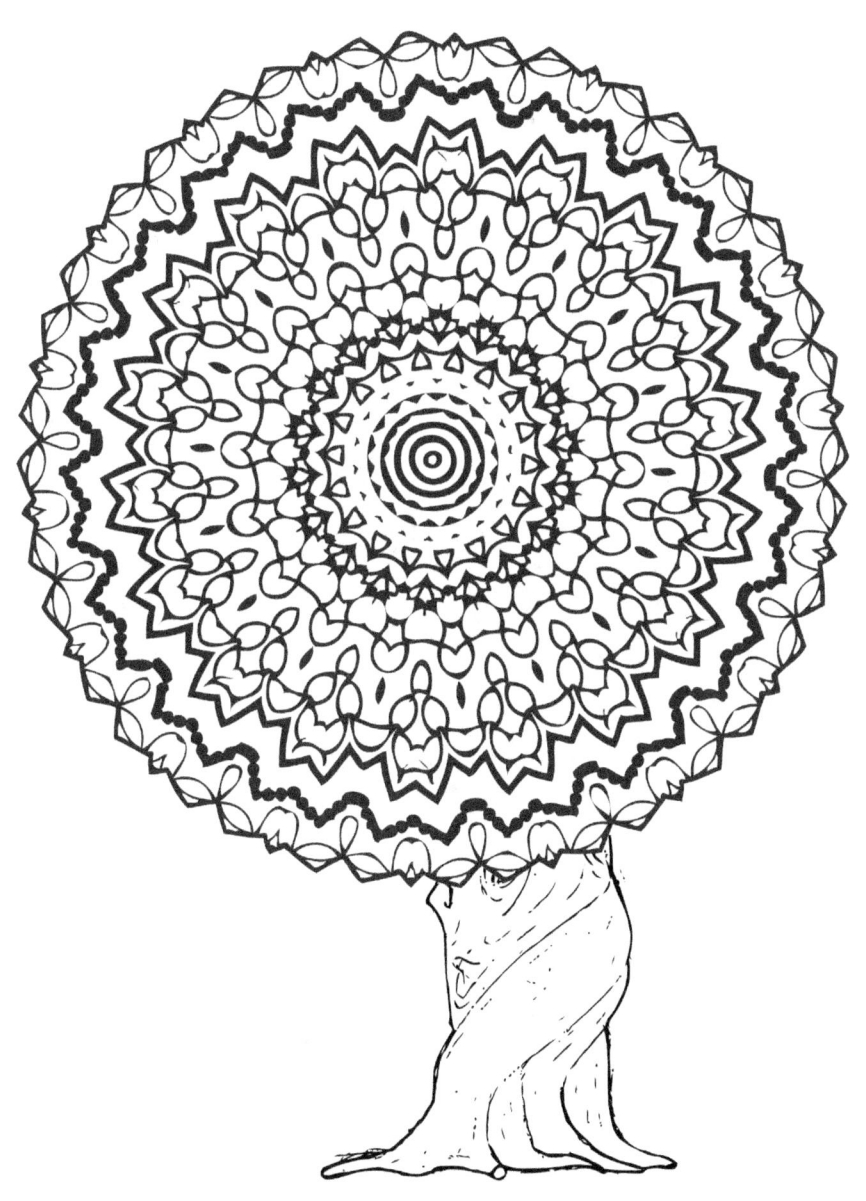

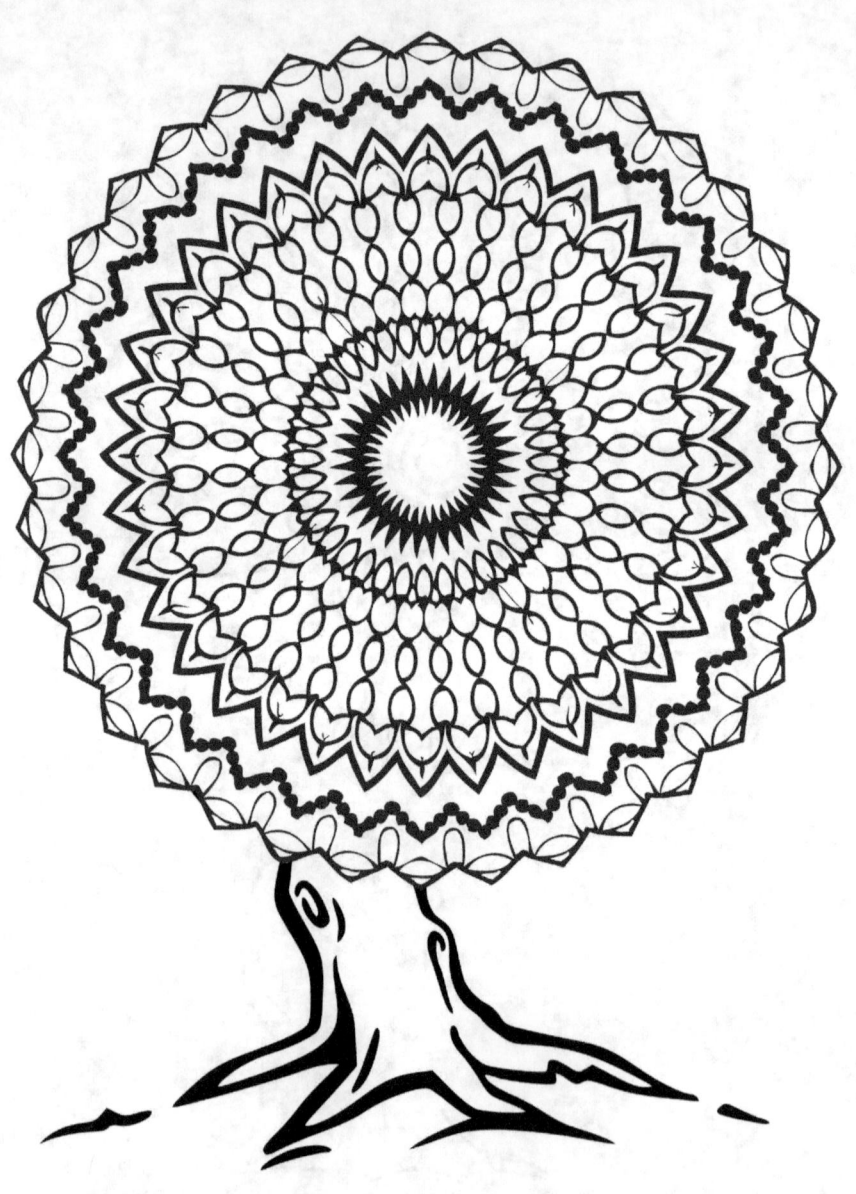

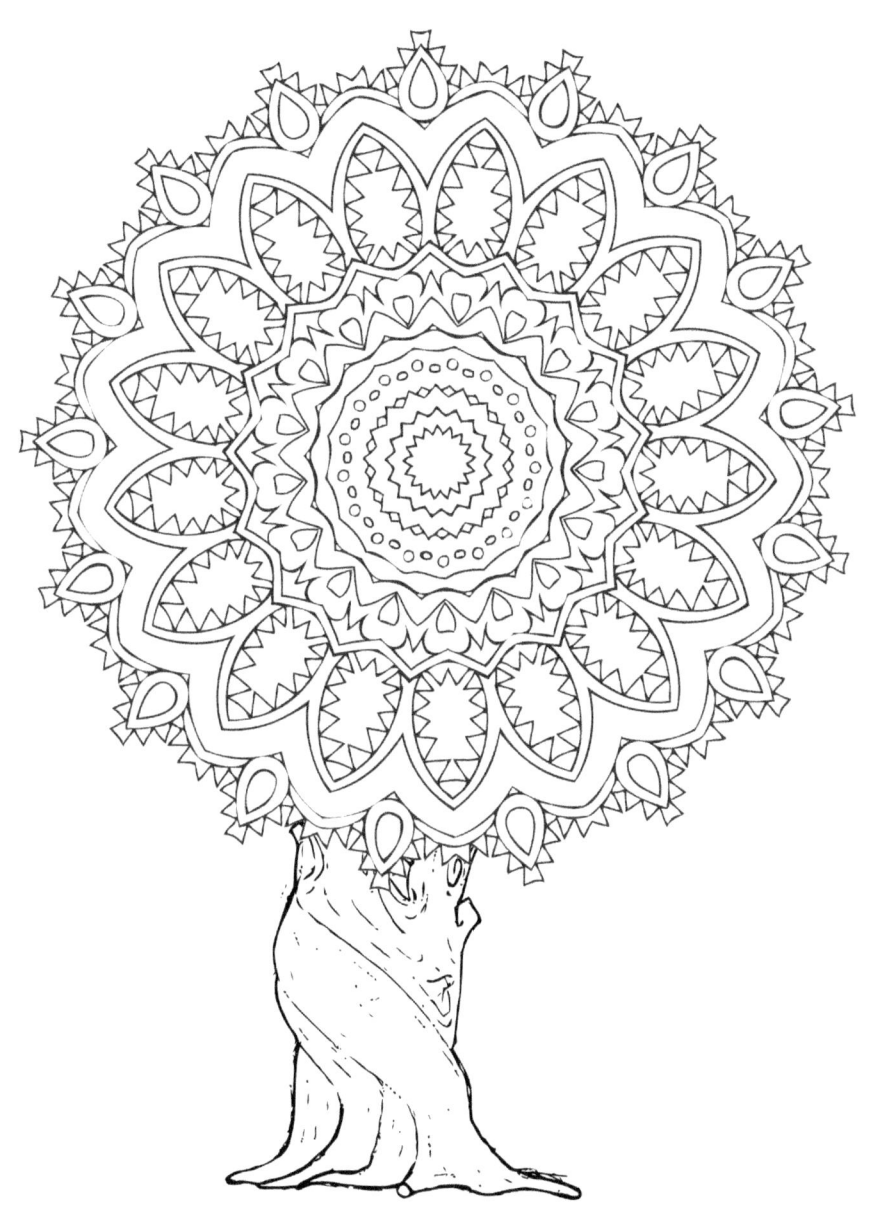

www.ingramcontent.com/pod-product-compliance
Lightning Source LLC
Chambersburg PA
CBHW061802280526
45787CB00003BA/1446